1983

POLICY STUDIES IN EMPLOYMENT

General Editor: Sar A. Levitan

Programs in Aid of the Poor

Third Edition

Sar A. Levitan

The Johns Hopkins University Press, Baltimore and London

This study was prepared under a grant from the Ford Foundation

The Johns Hopkins University Press, Baltimore, Maryland 21218
The Johns Hopkins Press Ltd., London

Originally published, 1973

Johns Hopkins paperback edition, 1973

Library of Congress Catalog Card Number 76–17234
ISBN 0–8018–1899–0 (hardcover)
ISBN 0–8018–1900–8 (paperback)

Contents

List of Figures

List of Tables

Map

Preface to the Third Edition

Programs in Aid of the Poor was originally prepared in 1965 for the National Commission on Technology, Automation, and Economic Progress and was published simultaneously by the commission, as part of its studies, and by the W. E. Upjohn Institute for Employment Research. The initial intention to merely update the study in 1969 became a complete revision reflecting the radical changes brought about in the American welfare system by the Great Society. Contrary to the popular image, the first Nixon administration continued to expand the earlier efforts in aid of the poor. But progress or new initiatives have been halted. As the nation is entering its third century, the debate is whether the efforts on behalf of the poor should continue or whether retrenchment is in order. The outcome is now a matter of national debate and of vital concern to one in every nine Americans, those classified as being poor.

The purpose of this study is to review and appraise existing programs in aid of the poor and to explore feasible approaches to the alleviation of poverty in the future. After examining the characteristics of the poor, the study summarizes the major antipoverty measures now in effect, focusing on the operation of the federal welfare system. The system is divided into four types of programs:

income maintenance programs aimed largely at aiding the poor who are outside the work force; programs supplying goods and services; programs whose immediate goal is to avert the spread of poverty to new generations; and programs to aid the working poor. The final chapter is devoted to a discussion of programs that might be adopted over the immediate years ahead.

Rather than clog the volume with references, the reader seeking source materials is invited to turn to the suggested readings at the end of each chapter. The excessive references to the author's other studies are not because they are the "best," but because *Programs in Aid of the Poor* is based on these studies and they offer the inquiring reader convenient sources to the materials used in the present volume.

I am indebted to my former and current colleagues at the Center for Social Policy Studies, Karen Alderman, William Johnston, David Marwick, Robert Taggart, and Gregory Wurzburg, for their contributions to this volume. Barbara Strong prepared the volume for publication.

The study was prepared under an ongoing grant from the Ford Foundation to the Center for Social Policy Studies, George Washington University. In accordance with the Foundation's practice, complete responsibility for the preparation of the volume was left to the author.

Sar A. Levitan
Center for Social Policy Studies
The George Washington University

Programs in Aid of the Poor

1

The Poor: Dimensions and Programs

If all the afflictions of the world were assembled on one side of the scale and poverty on the other, poverty would outweigh them all.

—Rabba, Mishpatim 31:14

INCOME INEQUALITY

"The poor shall never cease out of the land," according to the Bible. Rather than a pessimistic forecast, this prophecy is recognition that each society defines poverty in its own terms.

Poverty is a relative concept. It is primarily for this reason that in the richest country in the world, one person in nine can be designated as poor. In less affluent countries, poverty is equated with living at the brink of subsistence. In this country, even the lowest-income families are rarely confronted with the specter of starvation, though many are the victims of an inadequate diet.

Inequality is a problem in all societies in all times. No system distributes income evenly nor necessarily should it. The reasons for this inequality of incomes are many. Some are worthy and some are unconscionable, but the trends are remarkably constant. Income distribution today is little different from the pattern just after World War II. The poorest 20 percent of all families receive only about as much money income as the top 1 percent, and there

1

is some evidence that these figures may actually understate the full extent of inequality.

MEASURING POVERTY

Insofar as it can be measured, poverty can be defined as a lack of goods and services needed for an "adequate" standard of living. Because standards of adequacy vary both with the society's general level of well-being and public attitudes toward deprivation, there is no universally accepted definition of individual or family basic needs. The amount of money income necessary to provide for any agreed-upon set of basic needs is equally difficult to determine. For example, government programs such as free education, subsidized food, or medical care reduce the amount of cash required to support a family; and differentials in the cost of living between urban and rural areas, and among regions, raise the income requirements for some people and lower them for others. It is no wonder, then, that experts differ over the purchasing power that an individual or family needs for a minimum acceptable level of economic welfare.

Despite these conceptual and technical problems of measurement, the federal government has devised a poverty index which has gained wide acceptance. Developed by the Social Security Administration in 1964, this index is based on the cost of a minimum diet, estimated by the Department of Agriculture on the basis of a 1955 survey at about $1.33 per person per day in a four-member family with two school-age children (1976 prices). The total cost of living of the low-income family is estimated to be three times its food expenditures (with adjustments for changes in the level of consumer prices); thus, a larger family will have a proportionately higher poverty threshold. Farm families are presumed to need only 85 percent of the cash income required by nonfarm families, two-person families with an elderly head 10 percent less than those under 65 years of age, and households headed by females slightly less than other households. A summary of the federal government's definition of poverty income, based on 1976 prices, is presented by the following table:

2

Number of family members	Nonfarm	Farm
1	$3,000	$2,550
2	3,900	3,400
3	4,900	4,200
4	5,850	5,000
5	6,800	5,800
6	7,800	6,600

There are several flaws in this poverty index. First, the distinction between "nonfarm" and "farm" is extremely crude. It makes no allowance for regional variations in the cost of living or for higher prices in central cities, where many of the poor are concentrated. Set initially at 70 percent, the level for farm families was arbitrarily raised to the present level of 85 percent. Second, the food costs on which the budget is based were developed for "temporary or emergency use" and are inadequate for a permanent diet. For a family of four, an annual income of $5,850 provides only the barest subsistence. Also, the emphasis on cash income alone may yield paradoxical results. Because the income source is not a consideration, the poverty standard excludes those four-person families who earn $5,850 or more in cash, but whose disposable income after Social Security taxes and work expenses are deducted is below the poverty line. On the other hand, a family of four receiving only welfare payments of $5,850 or more during the year would not be poor. The exclusion of in-kind benefits and assets in determining the number of poor further detracts from the precision of the index. Nearly a tenth of the United States population, mostly poor persons, received food stamps in 1976. Finally, the assumption that a family needs two dollars for shelter, clothing and other needs for every food dollar (thus a poverty index three times the food budget) was based on the finding that in the 1950s the average consumer spent one-third of his income for food. More recent data indicate that this proportion has fallen to 28 percent, so the food budget might well be multiplied by 3.5, instead of 3, to derive the poverty level. A poverty line obtained in this way would be considerably higher than the "official" one. The pitfall of using a "stagnant" poverty level—one which adjusts only for price increases but not for productivity gains and the rising living standards of the American people—is also illustrated by the growing gap between the poverty level and median family income. The former rose only two-fifths between 1960 and 1974 while the latter more than doubled. In 1960 the median family income was 1.9 times the poverty level for a family of four. By 1974 it was 2.5 times as much.

A proposed solution is a flexible poverty line. One suggestion is to divide the median family income by two, thereby pegging the standard at three-fourths higher than the level set by the government. Because there has been little redistribution of income in recent years, a flexible index would indicate that our progress against poverty has been scant. For the present, however, the government poverty index is the most widely accepted and workable measure of poverty, and available data are gathered on this basis.

IDENTIFYING THE POOR

Measured by government statistics, poverty declined markedly in the decade of the 1960s. In 1960 nearly 40 million persons, or 22 percent of the population, were classified as poor by the government's poverty index. By 1969, this number had been reduced to approximately 24 million, or 12 percent of the population. Most of this progress occurred during the second half of the decade, when jobs were plentiful. The government-mounted special efforts to reduce poverty also helped. But during the subsequent five years no headway was made, and in 1974 the number of poor was still over 24 million (figure 1). But as noted earlier these data ignore the in-kind aid received by the poor. If the value of in-kind assistance had been included, the number of poor would have shown a further decline by 1974. Still, the problem of poverty persists, and the nation's increasing affluence makes the deprivation of those who remain poor both more noticeable and more poignant.

The incidence of poverty is related to age, color, sex of family head, work status, and educational attainment (table 1). Blacks are four times as likely as whites to be poor. Families headed by women are six times as likely to be poor as families headed by males. When the head of the family has eight years of schooling or

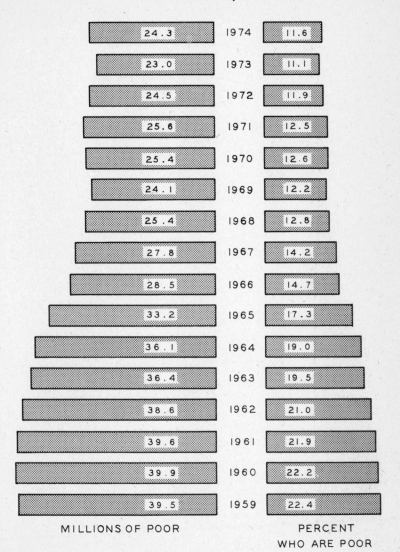

FIGURE I
POVERTY, 1959-74

MILLIONS OF POOR		PERCENT WHO ARE POOR
24.3	1974	11.6
23.0	1973	11.1
24.5	1972	11.9
25.6	1971	12.5
25.4	1970	12.6
24.1	1969	12.2
25.4	1968	12.8
27.8	1967	14.2
28.5	1966	14.7
33.2	1965	17.3
36.1	1964	19.0
36.4	1963	19.5
38.6	1962	21.0
39.6	1961	21.9
39.9	1960	22.2
39.5	1959	22.4

Source: U.S. Bureau of the Census

Table 1. Characteristics of the poor, 1974

	Persons in Families		Persons Living Alone	
Characteristic	Number (thousands)	Poor as percent of total in category	Number (thousands)	Poor as percent in total in category
Total	19,440	10	4,820	26
Age group		These are aggregate numbers which are not broken down for persons living in families and persons living alone.		
Under 16	9,320			16
16 to 64	11,632			9
65 and over	3,308			16
Race of family head				
White	3,482	7	3,773	23
Spanish origin	527	21	207	34
Black	1,530	28	961	41
Other	97	13	86	32
Family status				
Head	5,109	9	4,820	26
Related children	10,196	15	——	—
Others	4,135	6	——	—
Type of residence				
Central city	6,917	13	1,879	24
Outside central city	4,574	6	1,218	20
Farm	1,380	16	116	31
Other nonmetropolitan	6,569	12	1,607	34
Sex				
Male	10,877	6	1,607	20
Female	8,563	37	3,212	29
Work experience of family head				
Full-year, full-time	980	3	303	5
Part-time or part-year	1,711	16	1,382	29
Did not work	2,390	25	3,130	43
Armed forces	27	3	4	4
Education of family head				
8 or less	1,873	17	2,000	41
1-3 years high school	1,011	13	648	28
4 years high school	1,026	6	706	17
College, 1 year or more	466	3	518	12

Source: U.S. Bureau of the Census

less, the incidence of poverty is six times that for families headed by a person with some college education.

Overall changes in the number of poor mask the considerable movement of persons into and out of poverty (figure 2). That the total number of poor in 1969, for example, was slightly lower than in 1968 was the net effect of the movement out of poverty by 37 percent of the poor in that year while 34 percent of those classified as poor in 1969 were not in poverty during the previous year. Just as minority and female-headed units are more likely to be poor, they are also less likely to escape poverty. The proportion of 1968 poor also poor in 1969 varied from about half of the families headed by white males, to two-thirds of those headed by nonwhite males and white females, to three-fourths of the families headed by nonwhite females. Conversely, families headed by nonwhites and females were more likely to fall into poverty. A longitudinal study of 5,000 families by the University of Michigan Survey Research Center found that over a six year period only one in four of all poor families was counted as poor during the entire period.

For the purpose of this survey, the poor can be divided into four major groups: the elderly, working-age adults who are employed, those of working age who are not employed, and children in poor families. While these groups share the symptoms of low income, their problems vary and different programs are required to lift them out of poverty.

The Aged Poor

Of all age groups in the population, aged citizens have the highest incidence of poverty. One in every six persons aged 65 or older lived in poverty in 1974, compared with only one in nine persons under the age of 65. If anything, the situation may have been worse than these figures indicated, for the estimate of 3.3 million elderly poor excluded many living in public homes and more than 1 million others whose own income would have classified them among the poor but who lived in nonpoor households. There has been a dramatic drop in the number of aged poor—from 4.3 million in 1971 to 3.3 million in 1974. Credit is due largely to more generous social security benefits and the growth of private and

7

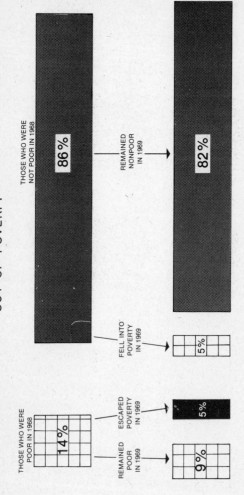

FIGURE 2

MOVEMENT INTO AND
OUT OF POVERTY

THOSE WHO WERE
NOT POOR IN 1968

86%

REMAINED
NONPOOR
IN 1969

82%

FELL INTO
POVERTY
IN 1969

5%

THOSE WHO WERE
POOR IN 1968

14%

ESCAPED
POVERTY
IN 1969

5%

REMAINED
POOR
IN 1969

9%

Source: Tabulations by Terence Kelly of the Urban Institute from
unpublished data, U.S. Bureau of Census

veterans' pensions. The supplemental security income program, begun in 1974 and not reflected in these data, may help further reduce the number of aged poor in the future. However, as the aged become more numerous in our society, the problems of meeting their income needs will intensify.

The major cause of poverty among the elderly is that few hold jobs. While some of the elderly poor are willing and able to work regularly, the vast majority cannot do so. Their infirmities are doubly critical because an increasing number of the elderly persons live alone and must provide for their own support. The best, and frequently the only, way to help these people is through some form of income support. Provision must also be made for high medical costs, which can be devastating for anyone living close to or below the poverty line.

Children in Poverty

At the other end of the age spectrum, nearly two of five persons classified as poor in 1974 were children under sixteen years of age, and one child in six lived in poverty. This fact is of special social concern because these children are almost inevitably denied opportunities from the very start and are thus impeded in preparing themselves for productive adult lives.

Many children live in poverty because they are its cause. That is, low-income families are frequently driven into poverty by the addition of family members. There is a close relationship between family size and poverty, with 54 percent of poor children coming from families with five or more members (figure 3). A higher incidence of poverty among larger families is to be expected in a society where need is ignored as a factor in wage determination, and where the necessity of child care often hinders the wife or female family head from earning needed income.

Poor children have special needs over and above those which can be provided by family income maintenance. Health care, compensatory education, and vocational training, in particular, are required to provide permanent exits from poverty.

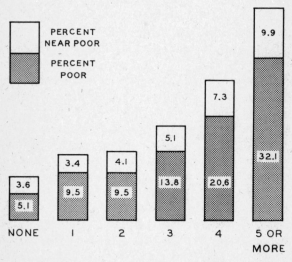

FIGURE 3
POVERTY AND FAMILY SIZE
1974

PERCENT
NEAR POOR

PERCENT
POOR

NUMBER OF CHILDREN UNDER 18

Source: U.S. Bureau of the Census

The Working Poor

Lack of employment is often the cause of poverty, but employment itself does not guarantee an adequate income. Over half of the 5.1 million poor family heads worked in 1974. Many single poor persons under 65 years of age were employed at least part time. For all these persons and their families, poverty was the result of low-paying jobs as well as intermittent unemployment and large families.

Though the problem is often overstated, unemployment remains a major cause of poverty. The poor are the victims of forced idleness more frequently than the nonpoor. Poor family heads, both male and female, are about three times as likely to be unemployed as are nonpoor family heads.

The majority of the working poor who do not experience unemployment encounter other labor market difficulties. Many leave the work force either voluntarily or because of illness or disability. An even greater number are employed at low-paying jobs. Only one-sixth of all family heads who worked were employed primarily as private household or other service workers, laborers, or farmers in 1974, but these occupations accounted for nearly half of the working poor family heads. In each of these occupations at least one family head in nine was in poverty. Over one-half of poor family heads and a third of single poor persons worked during 1974 but were not able to overcome poverty. About one-fifth of all poor families, in fact, had two or more persons working at some time during the year but remained poor. The number of family heads who worked full time year-round but remained poor declined steadily during the 1960s, and at a faster rate than the total poverty population, but in 1974 there remained 980,000 family heads, with about 4 million dependents, and another 303,000 unrelated individuals who were continuously employed but were still unable to work their way out of poverty.

For the working poor, then, the problems are frequent joblessness, low wages, and inadequate skills, all of which make the higher-paying jobs inaccessible. Manpower programs designed to smooth the operation of the labor market, enhance the productivity of low-income workers, and open opportunities for employment and advancement will alleviate the plight of the working poor. Effective enforcement of protective legislation to eliminate discrimination is also required while these manpower programs are being implemented.

The Nonworking Poor

Despite canards about the link between laziness and poverty, most of the unemployed working-age poor are simply not employable, either because of personal handicaps or because enough jobs are not available for them. Recent data on the reasons that poor people do not work indicate that illness and family responsibilities are the primary barriers. Of poor males aged 22 to 59 who did not work at all during 1974, more than three-fifths were ill or disabled. For male family heads, the percentage probably was higher. Seven out of ten females in this age group cited home responsibilities as the obstacle to outside work and almost one in five were ill or disabled. Thus, the presence of children not only increases income needs and the likelihood of poverty, but also hinders the employment of mothers and therefore reduces (or limits) the income available to meet family needs. Others were enrolled in school or training programs which would presumably enhance their employability, or had searched unsuccessfully for work. Some of the nonworking poor could and should be lured or goaded into employment; but for the vast majority of these poor, jobs are not the answer and some form of income support must be devised to help them escape deprivation.

STRATEGIES FOR HELPING THE POOR

Poor people need money. Whether they are young or old, their major immediate problem is the lack of income to purchase the most basic goods and services. But beyond this, the various categories of the poor have different needs, many of which cannot be filled with liberalized income support programs. Family heads and young people with their life's work ahead of them must have not only mere daily subsistence but also encouragement and support

12

for acquiring the skills sought by employers. For the aged, medical care and nursing homes are primary concerns. Children also need health care and the basic education to assure them opportunities in the future. For all poor people, direct provision of housing, medical care, food, and other goods and services can serve as a supplement to income maintenance.

Since the time of the New Deal, the United States has developed an intricate, though far from comprehensive, series of programs to assist the economically disadvantaged. The underlying assumption of this system is that special-purpose programs are required to take care of the diverse needs of the poor. Though some programs single out one of the four categories of the poor for special attention, other programs overlap in their coverage. It is therefore easier to classify the programs according to what they provide rather than by the groups they serve.

Types of Programs

Four types of programs are designed to aid the poor: (1) cash support, (2) direct provision of necessities such as food, shelter, and medical care, (3) preventive and compensatory efforts for children and youth, and (4) attempts to restructure existing institutions or help individuals adapt to those institutions.

Income maintenance programs are the major form of assistance to the poor. Because poverty is generally defined as the lack of adequate income, it can be most directly attacked by cash subsidies. To the extent that the family unit itself is the best, or at least the most appropriate, judge of how its limited resources should be allocated, income maintenance is a more acceptable form of assistance than the provision of goods and services.

The income subsidy approach is not without its inherent problems, however. One is the possibility that payments to employable persons will diminish their incentive to work. In addition, income subsidies may not be used for the intended purpose of providing basic sustenance. Finally, semantics plays a significant role. The public may agree to pay allowances to poor people as they undergo training, but may be unwilling to support relief for the unemployed.

13

Included among the existing cash income maintenance programs are Old Age, Survivors, and Disability Insurance (OASDI), unemployment insurance, public assistance, veterans' pensions, and workers' compensation. Because public sentiment against income payments to employable persons apparently remains strong, these programs are aimed for the most part at persons outside of the work force, or those who have been forced out of jobs. However, more comprehensive programs—such as guaranteed income, negative income tax, or family allowance—have been proposed to distribute income subsidies on the basis of need rather than labor force status.

Another group of programs provides goods and services directly to the needy, as a supplement to their cash income. Whatever the relative conceptual preferences between helping the poor with cash or in-kind income, political realities frequently dictate the latter. Public attention must usually be focused on a specific problem in order to mobilize society's resources. For example, increased food appropriations were forthcoming only after a highly publicized investigation of hunger in the late 1960s in the United States, and the resulting program was tailored to meet this specific problem. It would have been infinitely more difficult to gain additional support for direct cash payments to the poor, which might or might not have been used to purchase a better diet.

Not only is in-kind aid more palatable politically, but it is argued that the government is often a better judge of needs and priorities than the individual. Moreover, in some instances the necessary goods are simply not available in the market and direct provision is more effective. For example, the construction of low-cost housing is not profitable and cannot be provided to the poor without direct government action, particularly where racial discrimination is involved. To grant housing subsidies to the poor without increasing the supply of housing would simply raise rents on existing units. In a similar manner, the government, in some cases, can provide a wide variety of goods and services more efficiently than can the private sector because of the economies of large-scale enterprise.

Other services are provided directly by the government, not so much to make life easier for today's poor as to give their children a better chance to avoid poverty. Helping families to have no more children than they want is one of the most effective ways of eliminating poverty. It is also important to provide proper care for mother and child, so that the young will be healthy. The federal government also supports compensatory education programs for children of the poor from preschool to college.

Finally, programs aimed at restructuring institutions and improving the ability of the poor to work with these institutions are intended to eliminate the immediate causes of poverty rather than merely to mitigate its symptoms. For the most part, such programs are directed toward the employable poor, opening opportunities for them to free themselves from poverty. They tend to concentrate on economic institutions, although increasing recognition has been given to the fact that control over noneconomic institutions is often a prerequisite to economic opportunity.

These efforts can be divided into three groups: first, programs that seek to improve the individual's ability to compete in the labor market through training, placement, rehabilitation, and incentives to private employers to hire the disadvantaged; second, programs that attempt to restructure the labor market through minimum wage, public employment, and antidiscrimination efforts; third, programs designed to help redevelop depressed urban and rural areas—including Indian reservations—in order to bring employment opportunities to geographic "pockets of poverty."

In the end, of course, the several programs complement each other. Not only must we assuage today's poverty through cash and in-kind aid, but we must prevent it in the future by better preparing society's youth to fulfill their potential and by giving the poor a better chance in the job market. But it is always easy to isolate the impact of these programs upon beneficiaries. Birth control and maternal care may be designed primarily to give the young a better start in life, but they also leave the mother in better condition to contribute to her own support. Similarly, the differentiation between cash support and "rehabilitative" programs is often blurred

15

in reality. It is generally recognized, for example, that stipends must be paid to the poor if they are to undertake an effective training course.

Despite the rhetoric favoring cash assistance over in-kind aid, the trend in recent years has been in favor of the latter. In the 1970s, federal in-kind outlays have continued to expand and now exceed the traditional, federally aided and locally administered cash assistance programs. In 1974 federal outlays per poor person amounted to $1,197, but only 41 percent was in cash. A decade earlier, the annual assistance per poor person amounted to $320 (in 1974 dollars) and 81 percent was in cash.

Work and Welfare

Prevailing societal values often dictate that assistance programs be differentiated on the basis of the labor force status of recipients. Thus, programs aimed for the working poor may be distinguished from those designed to help people outside the labor force. This differentiation is becoming less important in developing further aid programs. The food stamp program, which became a major aid program during the 1970s, operates very much like a negative income tax, and there seems to be increasing acceptance of the advisability of efforts that do not attempt to make distinctions based on labor force status.

The inherent difficulties of categorizing the poor according to labor force status are obvious, and official government definitions of labor force offer only limited help. Many poor people move in and out of the labor force depending upon overall economic conditions and personal circumstances. There is an increasing awareness that society may be best served by supplementing the income of the working poor, and, conversely, by encouraging relief recipients to work without losing all or, at least, part of their public assistance. It is also difficult to decide *a priori* which individuals should be provided basic income through work (wages) and which should be provided support through public assistance. For example, should a female head of a family, with minor dependents and no regular income, be required to work for support or should the state assume the obligation of making direct contributions for her family's sustenance? Experts disagree over whether society would be better served by providing work for the mother—assuming jobs are available—or by providing sufficient income to allow the mother to devote full time to rearing her children. Those who favor the latter alternative would also redefine remunerative work to include childrearing.

Delivery of Services

Another problem in choosing antipoverty strategies is the administrative structure for the delivery of these services. As the 1960s opened, federal social programs were few and their budgets correspondingly slim. The federal government matched funds for public assistance and vocational education programs, but administration of these was largely left up to the states—even when the government supplied all of the funds, as it did in the case of employment services. One of the tenets of the Great Society, however, was to fund public and private local sponsors to implement national priorities, frequently bypassing involvement by elected state and local officials. It was assumed that federal expertise would be more efficiently applied to running the emerging new efforts aimed at combating poverty.

By the end of the 1960s, a reaction was building against the presumed unwieldiness of this apparatus. Grant-in-aid programs had proliferated and funds flowed from a variety of federal spigots. The result was often an uncoordinated tangle of programs in each locality, under the auspices of a maze of funding arrangements and operating guidelines.

To improve the delivery of services locally, proposals have been made for decentralization and decategorization of federal social programs. Both of these terms are generic, and connote a philosophy rather than a specific method. "Decentralization" generally refers to a decline in the federal role in administering programs, and a concomitant increase in state and local authority. "Decategorization" refers to a reduction in the earmarking of funds for specific purposes by Congress, in order to give states and localities broader choice of spending priorities. Just as each governmental unit faces unique problems, the argument goes, so should it

17

have the flexibility in committing resources and administering programs to meet these needs.

Congress enacted the first "revenue sharing" in 1972, by distributing to state and local governments about $6 billion a year, which could be used for a wide variety of purposes. But it is unrealistic to expect Congress to abdicate all responsibility for overseeing the funds that it raises, as would be required by complete decategorization and decentralization. In overhauling the numerous categorical employment and training efforts Congress rejected, in 1973, the administration's proposed revenue-sharing approach in favor of a federal-state-local partnership. The debate continues concerning the appropriate degree of federal control over its grants, the need for retaining national programs, and the ability of local officials to administer the programs. At present, however, the swing of the pendulum favors greater state and local responsibility.

THE SCALE OF ANTIPOVERTY EFFORTS

The various programs for the poor involve a substantial aggregate cost even though exact measurement is not possible because many programs serve the nonpoor as well as the poor. According to the latest estimates of the Community Services Administration, 1974 federal expenditures to help the poor amounted to some $27 billion (table 2). State and local expenditures might raise total governmental outlays by another 50 percent, with private, philanthropic efforts adding another billion dollars or more if the value of volunteer charitable work is included. While these are rough estimates, it is fair to say that in 1975 the total price tag of programs in aid of the poor amounted to about $42 billion.

This estimate includes payments made to poor people who participated in programs available to all, and not just the resources allocated on the basis of need. For example, the inclusion of Old Age, Survivors, Disability, and Health Insurance (OASDHI) as part of total welfare costs may be questioned by some because the program's eligibility test is based on prior contributions rather than personal need. But whatever the goals or criteria, all the programs

Table 2.   Federal aid to the poor, fiscal years 1964, 1970, and 1974.

Program	Fiscal (billions)		
	1964	1970	1974
Total	$7.7	$17.9	$27.0
Cash	6.2	8.8	11.9
OASDI and railroad retirement	3.8	5.2	6.3
Public assistance	1.3	2.2	3.8
Veterans' pensions and compensation	0.8	1.0	1.0
Unemployment benefits	0.3	0.2	0.6
Other	a	0.1	0.2
Employment and training	0.2	1.5	2.0
Community and economic development	a	0.6	0.8
Education	0.1	1.4	1.8
Health	0.7	4.0	6.2
Housing	0.1	0.3	0.8
Food	0.2	0.8	2.4
Child care and other social services	0.2	0.5	1.1

a Less than $50 million.
Note: Details may not add to totals because of rounding.
Source: U.S. Department of Commerce, *Statistical Abstract of the United States: 1975* (Washington: Government Printing Office, 1975), p. 405.

included in this survey provide needed assistance to the poor, raising some out of poverty and reducing its severity for many others.

No matter how much money and other resources American society contributes to its poor citizens, it is not possible to judge the adequacy of these contributions because no generally accepted criteria exist to suggest what percentage of the gross national product, or even of governmental expenditures, should be allocated to the poor. Nor are international comparisons of much help, since needs and programs among countries differ widely. In the last analysis, the level of expenditures probably depends upon the public tolerance of deprivation in light of the general standard of living. The assumption is that the United States has sufficient resources to reduce poverty even more rapidly than it did in the

1960s. The question is whether the rapid reduction of poverty can be made a primary and pressing national goal. The experience of the first half of the 1970s offers little hope that poverty will be eliminated in the United States in the near future.

ADDITIONAL READINGS

Ferman, Louis A. et al. (ed.). *Poverty in America*, revised edition. Ann Arbor: The University of Michigan Press, 1968.

Lampman, Robert J. *Ends and Means of Reducing Income Poverty.* Chicago: Markham Publishing Co., 1971.

Levitan, Sar A. and Taggart, Robert. *The Promise of Greatness.* Cambridge, Mass.: Harvard University Press, 1976.

Miller, Herman P. *Rich Man, Poor Man.* New York: Thomas Y. Crowell, 1972.

Poverty and Human Resources offers a complete review of the literature on poverty.

Stein, Bruno. *On Relief: The Economics of Poverty and Public Welfare.* New York: Basic Books, 1971.

U.S. Bureau of the Census. *Characteristics of the Low-Income Population.* Current Population Reports, Series P-60, latest year.

2

Cash Support Programs

You shall open wide your hand to your brother, to the needy,
and to the poor.

—Deuteronomy 15:11

In 1975 about one of every three Americans received assistance
from public programs. The total cost was about $175 billion, four-
fifths of which was paid in cash. The poor are much more likely to
receive cash transfer payments than are the nonpoor (figure 4).
And many of the nonpoor would have been poor without these
transfers. An estimated 6.4 million persons were kept out of poverty in 1971 by cash transfers.

The Social Security Act, the product of four decades of evolution since its enactment in 1935, is the most significant income
maintenance program for both the poor and the nonpoor. Programs contained in this act accounted for nine-tenths of the income support for the poor and for two-thirds of the payments to
the nonpoor. Two groups of programs established by the act were:
(1) social insurance programs—including Old Age, Survivors, and
Disability Insurance and unemployment insurance—both of which
distribute payments on the basis of prior earnings and prior tax
contributions; and (2) public assistance programs—for the elderly, the blind, the disabled, and families with dependent children
—which provide income support on the basis of need alone.

FIGURE 4
SOURCES OF INCOME, POOR AND ALL FAMILIES
1974

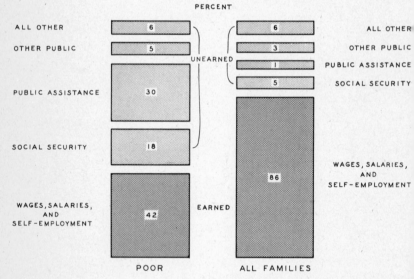

PERCENT

ALL OTHER — 6 — UNEARNED

OTHER PUBLIC — 5

PUBLIC ASSISTANCE — 30

SOCIAL SECURITY — 18

WAGES, SALARIES, AND SELF-EMPLOYMENT — 42 — EARNED

POOR

ALL OTHER — 6

OTHER PUBLIC — 3

PUBLIC ASSISTANCE — 1

SOCIAL SECURITY — 5

WAGES, SALARIES, AND SELF-EMPLOYMENT — 86

ALL FAMILIES

Source: U.S. Bureau of the Census

OASDI

Old Age, Survivors, and Disability Insurance distributes more income to the poor than any other government transfer program. One poor family in four receives these benefits. In addition, these income supports have prevented many households from falling into poverty. However, eligibility and benefit levels are determined *not* by recipients' current income but by their past contributions.

The social security system is vast, with total expenditures of $88 billion in fiscal 1976 including $16.6 billion paid for hospital and medical insurance. Some 32 million persons—one American in seven—received regular cash payments. Coverage is extensive: nine of every ten people in paid employment or self-employment are covered; of those who reached age 65 in 1972, only 7 percent were not eligible for some benefits; 95 percent of all children and their mothers would receive benefits if the father were to die.

Both the benefits and the burden of OASDI fall disproportionately on the bottom of the income spectrum. The program is financed by an 11.7 percent tax (including 2 percent for health insurance) on annual earnings up to $15,300 in 1976 shared equally by an employee and his employer. To the extent that the employer's contributions are part of the worker's defined earnings, the total tax amounts to about one dollar of every nine of the employee's compensation. Furthermore, there are no exemptions for the lowest-paid workers or for those with large families, therefore making the tax a relatively heavier burden on large poor families.

On the other hand, lower-income workers benefit disproportionately. A full covered single retiree with average monthly insured earnings of $750 would have received monthly benefits equal to 53 percent of that amount in 1974; a retiree with earnings of $400 would have received 65 percent in benefits; and a retiree with $100 in monthly earnings would have received 121 percent. The highest-paid worker would have paid more than six times as much in tax contributions but would have received benefits only three times as great.

The extent to which OASDI should redistribute income is

23

widely debated, but it now does so in two ways. It transfers money from the higher-paid retiree to the lower-paid retiree by granting relatively more generous benefits to the latter. It also transfers money from the generation now working to the retired generation. OASDI is said to be an "insurance" system, but unlike a commercial insurance company, which invests premiums to pay for future claims, the federal government collects only enough in taxes to finance current expenditures and keeps in the "trust fund" an amount equal to only one year's benefits.

Computation of benefits depends upon age of retirement, spouse's eligibility for benefits, the number and age of survivors eligible to receive benefits, and the level of covered earnings. The minimum requirement for benefits is generally six quarters during which wages equalled at least $50. Workers with 40 quarters of coverage are fully insured. Two exceptions are: a minimum benefit of $69 per month for persons who reached age 72 even if they had no covered work, and a minimum benefit of $101 for workers with prolonged years of covered employment at low wages.

Social security benefits are not means-tested, but they can be reduced if the recipient continues to work. For beneficiaries under 72, payments are reduced 50 cents for each dollar of earnings above $2,760. "Earnings" are considered income from labor, but not income from rents, royalties, or dividends. According to this, a beneficiary under 72 loses one dollar of every two above $2,760 in wages or salaries but income from interest, dividends, or gains made in the stock market do not affect social security benefits.

Although OASDI has continued to expand, several flaws remain in coverage and benefits. Some 7 percent of those between 65 and 72 years of age are not eligible for benefits. There remains the inequity that a wife's earnings effect a higher family retirement income only if they are larger than 50 percent of the husband's benefits. Finally, despite several recent increases, benefits remain inadequate to raise all recipients above the poverty threshold. In December 1975 some 8 percent of cash beneficiaries age 65 and over also received means-tested welfare supplemental security payments. The average monthly benefit of $207 in December 1975 left the retired worker just short of escaping poverty, but the average retired couple received benefits 15 percent above the poverty level (figure 5). An individual with the minimum benefit for persons covered because of earnings would receive $101.40 per month, less than half the poverty level. To protect the income of retired workers from inflation, the law provides that benefits be adjusted when the cost of living rises by at least 3 percent in one year. While social security is the single most important program for reducing poverty, it is not the most cost-effective approach, even for the aged.

Old age insurance provides income to a steadily rising portion of the aged population—up to 93 percent in 1975. Workers receive their full entitlement at age 65, but they can claim benefits earlier with a corresponding permanent decrease in the amount. At age 62, the earliest age to retire, the reduction is 20 percent. Because many of those who choose lower benefits were forced into early retirement by job loss or disability, and because they typically earned less than workers who wait until age 65, the permanent reduction in benefits is harsh. On the other hand, workers can increase their benefits by 1 percent for each year beyond 65 they postpone retirement.

Survivors insurance is payable to an insured worker's surviving children under 18 years of age (under 22 if they attend school), to the mothers of these children, to dependent parents, and to widows or dependent widowers. Finally, disability insurance provides for severely disabled but noninstitutionalized adults (age 18 to 64) who cannot find substantial gainful employment. To be eligible for insurance payments, they must have worked at least 20 of the 40 quarters prior to disability; or, in the case of workers disabled before age 24, they must have worked half of the quarters (but not fewer than six) since turning 21. Disability benefits are paid after a waiting period of five months, and medical proof of disability is required, along with a determination that the disability rules out gainful employment. About one-third of the estimated 7.5 million severely disabled adults receive disability insurance.

FIGURE 5
SOCIAL SECURITY BENEFITS
DECEMBER 1975

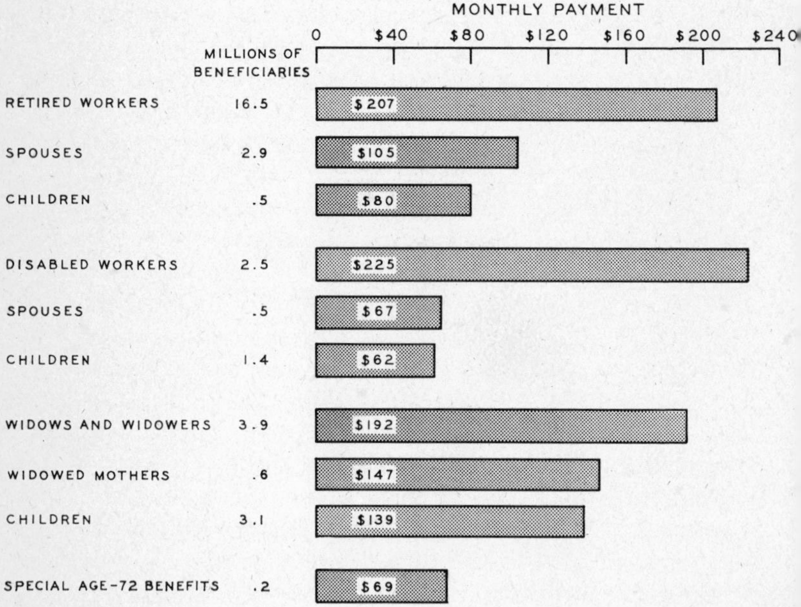

MONTHLY PAYMENT

	MILLIONS OF BENEFICIARIES	Monthly Payment
RETIRED WORKERS	16.5	$207
SPOUSES	2.9	$105
CHILDREN	.5	$80
DISABLED WORKERS	2.5	$225
SPOUSES	.5	$67
CHILDREN	1.4	$62
WIDOWS AND WIDOWERS	3.9	$192
WIDOWED MOTHERS	.6	$147
CHILDREN	3.1	$139
SPECIAL AGE-72 BENEFITS	.2	$69

Source: U.S. Department of Health, Education, and Welfare

PUBLIC ASSISTANCE

In addition to distributing benefits under OASDI to insured workers or their survivors, the Social Security Act provides Aid to Families with Dependent Children (AFDC) and assistance to the aged, blind, and disabled through the Supplemental Security Income (SSI) program. Persons not eligible under one of these federally-aided programs may receive state- and locally-funded general assistance. Of these programs, AFDC is by far the largest, constituting nearly seven-tenths of the 16.5 million recipients in late 1975 and well over half of the nearly $16 billion in fiscal 1976 expenditures. AFDC is identified with "welfare" because it accounted for most of the increase in means-tested income support after World War II (figure 6).

SSI generally offers substantially higher benefits than do AFDC and general assistance. Although public assistance lifts many persons out of poverty, nearly half of the families reporting public assistance income in 1974 were poor despite this aid.

Aid to Families with Dependent Children

By far the largest, costliest, and most controversial public assistance program is Aid to Families with Dependent Children. In late 1975 there were approximately 11.3 million recipients, including 8.1 million children, or more than one child in every ten. Benefits paid during that year totaled about $9 billion.

Though the federal government contributes more than half of the total cost of AFDC, it delegates administration of the program to the states, within broad federal guidelines. The federal government pays about five-ninths of AFDC costs, state governments pay one-third, and local governments pay one-ninth. Most important, the states determine eligibility standards and the level of benefits. The grant paid to the recipient is based on need standards determined by each state, and may vary widely from state to state. The standard nominally reflects the cost of rent, utilities, food, clothing, and other basic expenses. In many states, however, there is little correlation between actual living costs and the established need standards. The monthly cost of basic needs calculated by the states

27

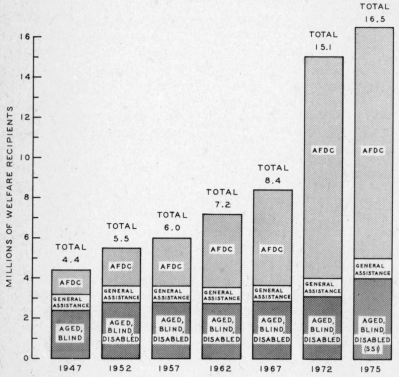

FIGURE 6
AFDC ACCOUNTED FOR MOST OF THE
WELFARE INCREASE AFTER WORLD WAR II

Source: U.S. Department of Health, Education, and Welfare

for a family of four on AFDC in 1975 ranged from $187 to $455 (excluding Alaska and Hawaii); the median was $322. But many states fail to pay even these low standards under AFDC. Varying rules determine the difference between need and public assistance payments. Only nineteen states pay up to the full amount under AFDC. Others set maximum benefits that are below standard needs or pay only a fixed percentage of the standard. In eleven states the amount paid is less than two-thirds of the minimum standards. Considering the stinginess of "standard need" definitions, the failure to make up this deficit leaves most public assistance recipients in deprivation. The average state maximum payment was $274. States with relatively low per capita income tend to pay lower benefits. In 1974 no state paid high enough benefits to keep an AFDC family out of poverty if it had no other income or in-kind assistance. The accompanying map shows the range of benefit levels and the parsimoniousness of some states (map 1).

AFDC growth since World War II has been substantial—doubling each decade between 1947 and 1967 and again between 1967 and 1972, when the expansion virtually ceased as the bulk of female-headed poor families qualified for assistance. That AFDC rose so rapidly during the 1960s was especially remarkable since the poverty population declined during that decade. The reasons for the expansion of AFDC are many and complex. Not only did more people become eligible, but the benefits were also increased and the stigma attendant to welfare was reduced.

There was considerable population growth in the quarter century after World War II, especially among children. But perhaps more important were changes in family structure resulting in an increasing number of households headed by women who are potential AFDC recipients. Not only did the rate of divorce increase 50 percent during the 1960s, but the number of children involved per divorce decree also increased. Although data are imprecise for desertions and separations without court decree—the "poor man's divorce"—these, too, became more numerous. Out-of-wedlock births multiplied from one in twenty to one in ten. But cause and effect cannot readily be disentangled. AFDC may be viewed as a

29

MAP I

MONTHLY AFDC PAYMENTS PER PERSON, NOV. 1975

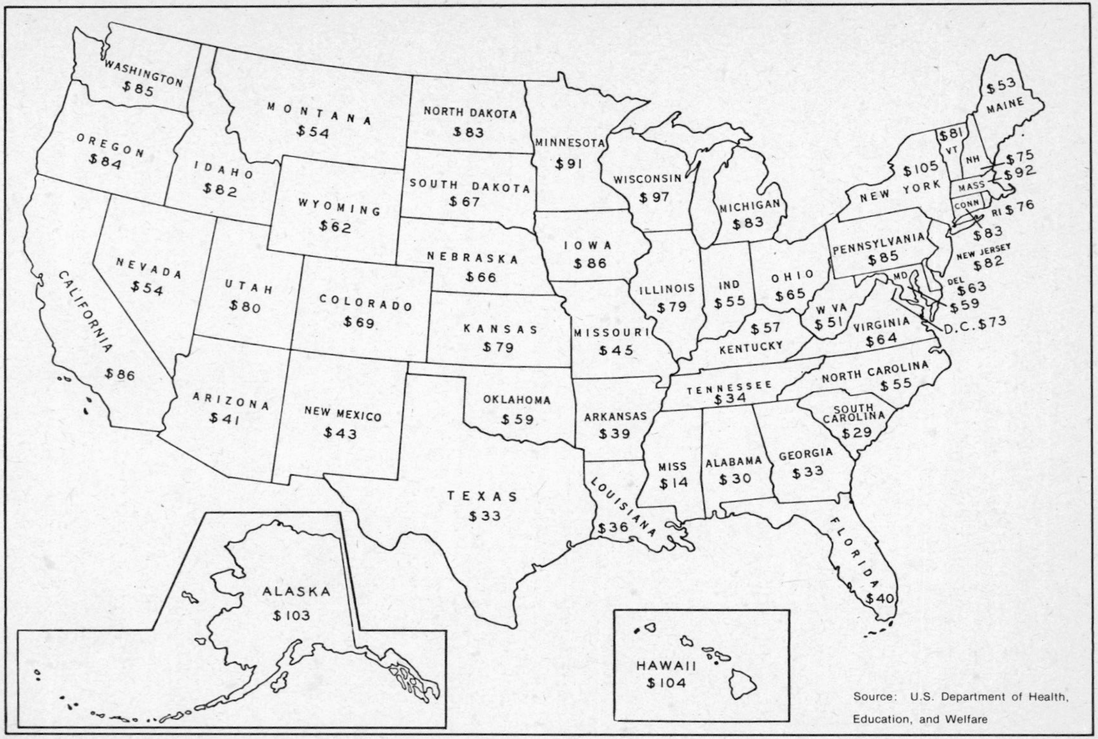

Source: U.S. Department of Health,
Education, and Welfare

response to economic and social pressures resulting from the rise of the single-parent family, but the program itself may induce families to modify their behavior in order to qualify for benefits. AFDC may encourage the very phenomenon to which it is a response, by inducing an unemployed man either to desert his family to make his dependents eligible for assistance or to fail to marry the mother. However, charges that mothers on welfare have additional children in order to qualify for higher payments remain unsubstantiated and many AFDC mothers seek and practice birth control when it is made available. The average AFDC family has 3.6 persons, and over three-fourths of the families have three or fewer children.

Supreme Court decisions and federal legislation have added to the welfare population by extending coverage to groups not previously eligible. In 1961 Congress allowed states to grant assistance to families that were dependent because of the unemployment of an employable parent. This "unemployed father" component, now available in 27 states, is restricted by federal regulations to those working fewer than 100 hours per month, no matter how meager their earnings. Most important was that 1967 provision to disregard $30 per month plus work expenses and one-third of additional earnings. In 1968 the court struck down the "man in the house" rule, which held a man living in an AFDC home responsible for the children's support even if he was not legally liable. The following year the Supreme Court invalidated residency requirements for public assistance. Later, states were permitted to grant aid to children after age 18 who were attending school. Income disregards—whereby states ignore certain earnings in computing eligibility and payments—have permitted many families who would otherwise have been disqualified to remain on the rolls.

While these developments increased the number of persons eligible for assistance, neighborhood legal services agencies, the welfare rights organizations, and other groups publicized the availability of, and eligibility requirements for, AFDC benefits. Improvements in the administration of assistance attracted more applicants as the wait between application and approval was shortened.

Finally, a basic condition for growth was the broader attractiveness of AFDC relative to other sources of income. As the federal government assumed a larger share of the burden, states became less reluctant to qualify individuals for aid and to provide more adequate benefits. Between 1947 and 1962 average AFDC payments and spendable average weekly earnings of all private employees rose equally; but between 1963 and 1975 the AFDC payment increased 123 percent while earnings barely doubled. And significant increases in the use of food stamps and medical care—not reflected in the cash payments—tilted the balance even more in the favor of welfare. (These in-kind income supplements are discussed in chapter 4.) Although working may still provide more income than public assistance alone to many families on welfare, combining these two sources may be preferable to either. In addition to the higher measurable benefits of welfare, the stigma of "being on relief" probably declined. Government income support became much more widely distributed, reaching a third of the population in 1975. AFDC recipients alone constitute more than one-tenth of the populations of New York City, Philadelphia, Baltimore, Boston, St. Louis, New Orleans, and the District of Columbia.

These forces, and the economic slowdown in 1969, contributed to the trebling of AFDC between 1961 and 1971. But public reaction against welfare, state cutbacks in benefits, and the imposition of new work requirements on recipients arrested the growth in the rolls during 1972. There was little growth through 1975. Although the administration officials attributed this leveling-off to better management, others believe that most eligible persons had already joined the aid rolls.

AFDC recipients are disadvantaged in many ways, but they are not a class unto themselves. According to a 1973 survey, fathers were present in only one AFDC home in eight, and three-fifths of these men were disabled. Nearly half of the families were non-white, but this proportion remained unchanged during the 1960s. AFDC mothers had substantially lower educational attainment than other women of the same age level: about twice as many had completed eight or fewer years of school. Their work experience also had serious limitations. Nearly one-fourth had never been employed, and of those who had worked, nearly half had been in private household and other service jobs, which generally provide meager earnings. The average number of children per family was 2.6, but nearly half of the families included at least one child born out of wedlock.

The outlook of AFDC families was not completely bleak. As their numbers increased, AFDC recipients' characteristics and aspirations became increasingly similar to the rest of the population's. More than one-quarter of the mothers were either working or looking for work, and this proportion was slowly rising. Their educational attainment, although still relatively low, was also rising. More had some paid work experience. Most significantly, studies have shown that AFDC recipients are no less eager to work than the rest of the population. In fact, since 1969 they have had a general incentive to supplement their income through earnings because the law provided that work expenses and the first $30 of earnings, plus one-third of additional earnings, could be disregarded in computing welfare benefits. Before 1969, many states had reduced benefits dollar-for-dollar as earnings increased; this "100 percent tax" certainly stifled incentives to seek work and to improve family income.

Although the "$30 and ⅓" incentive is part of federal law, the total amount of earnings which are ignored (or disregarded) in computing the assistance check varies from state to state. Some jurisdictions are very liberal in computing work expenses, while others are strict. Because of the spread in payment levels, the hourly earnings level required to remove a family of four from AFDC is more than $3.00 in many states. There are not many AFDC mothers who could qualify for such jobs—assuming they are available—and continue working full-time, year-round, and thus work their way off the welfare rolls.

Although the employability of many AFDC mothers is limited, it has become more acceptable for a female family head to work and child care facilities are expanding. It is thus no accident that, for more and more recipients, work and welfare go together. Just as poverty is often transitory, most families do not languish forever

33

on welfare. In recent years, as many as three-tenths of new cases left the public assistance rolls within a year and three-fifths closed within three years. And in 1974 one AFDC family in three had previously been on the rolls.

There can also be an inequity between families on welfare and those not on the rolls, because the work incentive applies only to those who are already receiving assistance. Thus, in a state whose eligibility level is $220 per month, a woman earning $240 would not qualify. But if her neighbor had already qualified for aid and then took a job paying $240 per month, the neighbor would keep not only all the earnings but at least $100 of her assistance check [$30 plus ⅓ ($240 − $30)], for a total income of $340. This incentive, paradoxically, may encourage some working poor family heads to quit their jobs, seek welfare, and then resume working. Combining work and welfare can be much preferable to drawing on either source alone.

But despite the increasing tendency to treat work and welfare as complements, three-fifths of the families who remained poor in 1974 had earned income. Only two-fifths of all poor families in 1974 were on welfare. Welfare alone was rarely adequate to raise a family above poverty, and only two-fifths of all poor families depended exclusively on welfare.

Supplemental Security Income

For nearly four decades assistance programs for the aged, blind, and disabled operated much as did AFDC. Although the federal government contributed a share of the cost, state and local governments largely determined eligibility and benefit levels, and administered the programs. Benefits were more generous than under AFDC, but they too varied widely.

Social security amendments passed in 1972 thoroughly revamped this system. In July 1975 the federal government guaranteed the aged, blind, and disabled a monthly income of $158 for an individual and $237 for a couple under the Supplemental Security Income (SSI) program. This represented an increase in benefits paid by nearly half the states. Even so, the guarantee equaled only about 70 percent of the poverty level for individuals and 82 percent for couples. States can supplement the federal guarantee, but without federal contributions. The law also provided that $20 per month of social security payments or other income, plus $65 of earned income and half of additional earnings, be disregarded in computing eligibility. It is ironic that the aged, blind, and disabled—whose ability to work is probably limited—have much more attractive incentives than do recipients of AFDC, many of whom can and should be encouraged to work. One explanation of the congressional generosity is the anticipation that in the case of these groups the liberal incentives carried a very low price tag.

The law substituted federal eligibility standards to the aged, blind, and disabled. The demeaning "declarations of indebtedness" required by many states to ensure that only the most destitute received benefits were eliminated. A lien on a welfare recipient's property netted little for the state but took a heavy toll in self-respect. The federal law, nonetheless, retained stringent standards. Aside from a home, an automobile, property for self-support, and life insurance policies worth less than $1,500, the assets of aged, blind, or disabled public assistance recipients could not exceed $1,500 for an individual or $2,250 for a couple. The intent of the law was to protect the taxpayer from the claims of those not in need, without debasing the recipient.

Congress expected these changes to channel more income to the aged, blind, and disabled. Program costs increased from $3.2 billion in fiscal 1972 (under the three separate programs) to an estimated $5.7 billion in fiscal 1976, including $1.2 billion in benefits paid by 28 states. The average monthly number of recipients rose from 3.1 million in fiscal 1972 to 4.3 million by the end of 1975.

The transition from local to federal administration of SSI was accompanied by the traditional problems that characterized locally administered welfare programs—high administrative costs and eligibility conflicts. Many of the expected benefits of federalization were slow to be realized.

Experience under the previous, separate programs showed that the number of aged recipients had declined by more than a quarter since its peak in 1950. At the beginning of 1973, there were about 2 million recipients. Similarly, the number of blind recipients had declined to some 80,000. Aid to the disabled, however, began only in 1951 and the number of recipients had increased steadily to the 1.2 million mark by 1973. The sharp decline in the first category was generally attributed to the spread of the social security system. As the number of aged welfare recipients dropped from 2.8 million in 1950 to 1.9 million in 1973, the number of OASDI recipients aged 65 and over grew from 1.8 million to 14 million. And the proportion of old age assistance recipients who also received OASDI climbed steadily to 63 percent.

Aged, blind, and disabled recipients of aid were likely to be old, white, and female:

	Median age	Proportion white	Proportion female
Aged	76	74%	68%
Blind	60	68	53
Disabled	55	68	55

These rolls were fairly stable: the mean duration on assistance was over five years for the aged and six years for the blind; that it was under three years for the disabled is partly due to the rapid growth of this program.

The aged were typically alone and without other support. Only one-quarter were living with their spouses, and only one-fifth were living with a son, daughter, or other relative. Fewer than 4 percent had children contributing regularly to their support. Their capacity for self-support was meager, not at all surprising among a population with an average age of 76 and one of every three above age 80 years. Of every ten recipients, nearly three had never worked and five more had not worked within five years. Of the 22 million persons 65 years of age and over in 1974, nearly one in seven, or 3.3 million, were poor. The number of aged poor had declined by one million in the preceding three years largely as a result of higher welfare benefits, including social security, supplementary security income, and veterans' benefits.

Nearly one of every four blind persons on public assistance lived alone. Remarkably, 8 percent were working full- or part-time, and one-fourth could travel outside the home unaided. But fully one-third had never worked. In addition to lack of vision, more than two-fifths had one or more chronic health problems.

The disabled were afflicted by a variety of impediments, both mental and physical. One-third lived in a household with no one else. The proportion of recipients who were confined dropped by half during the last decade to 15 percent. One of every seven recipients of disability insurance participated in vocational rehabilitation.

The aged, blind, and disabled are considered less capable of self-support and less responsible for their dependency than are AFDC recipients, and are hence deemed more "deserving" of aid. This public judgment is clearly reflected in notably higher benefits and more humane administration.

General Assistance

For the needy who do not qualify for federally supported aid, all states provide varying coverage and benefits through general assistance. Some provide cash payments; others provide only medical care, hospitalization, or burial. In Pennsylvania and New York in late 1975, there was one general assistance beneficiary for every five recipients of AFDC; in Alabama, one for every 3,200. The average monthly payment per recipient ranged from $10 in Oklahoma to $143 in the District of Columbia.

General assistance cases are concentrated in large cities. Monthly benefits in these cities in September 1974 were about $21 higher per recipient than the national average of $93; seventeen cities contained nearly half of all recipients. The total number of general assistance recipients has fluctuated considerably over the years, typically rising during economic slumps. Because of rapid turnover, there may be twice as many recipients during a year as at any given time.

Veterans' Assistance

Income support on a preferential basis has long been available to a selected segment of the population—the 29.6 million veterans and their families who comprised over two-fifths of the total population in 1975. This type of income support predates even the Revolutionary War. Colonial laws mandated public support for men incapacitated in defense of the community. Although present programs do not provide enough support to permit all veterans and their dependents to escape poverty, they go a long way toward providing basic needs, particularly for older veterans and indigent survivors of deceased veterans.

Two types of cash benefits, compensation and pensions, are provided. The cost to the federal government in 1976 was over $7.7 billion (figure 7). Compensation is paid to veterans (or their dependents) for an injury, disability, or death incurred while serving in the armed forces, and pensions are paid to war veterans (or their dependents) whose annual income is below a specified level and who are permanently and totally disabled. In practice the disability qualifications for a pension are relaxed as the veteran advances in age. The pension qualifications are more stringent for veterans below the age of 55, but veterans aged 65 and over may qualify on the basis of need. Altogether about one-fifth of total cash payments to veterans go to poor people.

Compensation

One of every thirteen veterans received compensation in 1976 for service-connected disability at a total cost to the government of $3.8 billion. Individual annual compensation averaged $1,900 ranging from $420 for a 10 percent disability to $7,860 for total disability. The payment to 50 percent or more disabled veterans is supplemented for dependents. Additional special compensation paid to veterans who suffered total blindness, deafness, or loss of limbs may boost the payment to $21,582 annually.

Congress periodically raises the level of compensation benefits to keep pace with rising living costs. Average annual compensation costs are likely to increase somewhat even in the absence of a rise

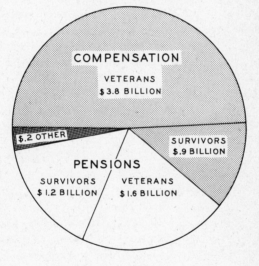

FIGURE 7
VETERANS INCOME SUPPORT
1976

TOTAL - $7.7 BILLION

COMPENSATION
VETERANS
$3.8 BILLION

$.2 OTHER

SURVIVORS
$.9 BILLION

PENSIONS

SURVIVORS
$1.2 BILLION

VETERANS
$1.6 BILLION

Source: U.S. Veterans Administration

in benefits because service-connected disabilities tend to become aggravated with advancing age. However, the higher mortality rate of injured men diminishes the potential rise in benefits if the men were to live out their normal life span. Four of every ten World War II veterans who were receiving compensation in 1976 qualified for only minimum disability benefits (10 percent impairment), compared with almost one of every seven World War I veterans. At the other extreme, 12 percent of World War I veterans who were receiving compensation were totally disabled, compared with 4.5 percent of World War II veterans. Because older veterans are more likely to suffer severe impairment, the average monthly compensation for World War I veterans was significantly higher than for World War II veterans—$197 as compared to $134.

Data are not available on the income level of veterans receiving service-connected compensation. However, a 1971 study found that veterans receiving compensation had lower annual incomes than their nondisabled peers, and many of the disabled would have been counted among the poor had they not received compensation. This is particularly true of the nearly 478,000 (out of a total of 2.2 million) whose degree of impairment was 50 percent or more. Many of these disabled veterans were probably unable to hold full-time jobs.

A total of $868 million in survivors benefits was distributed in 1976 among 506,000 dependents of servicemen who died as the result of military service. Benefits are provided under dual programs; death compensation, in effect prior to 1957, is paid to over one-fourth of the cases, and dependency and indemnity compensation is received by three-fourths of the cases. Eligibility for the latter benefits is not means-tested with the exception since 1957 of qualifying dependent parents.

Death compensation pays a flat annual rate of $1,044 to a widow and $1,452 to a widow with one dependent child. A dependent parent receives $900 annually and, unlike dependency and indemnity compensation for parents, payment is not means-tested or reduced in relation to other income.

Rates of dependency and indemnity compensation vary with the rank held by the deceased serviceman. Annual stipends range from

$2,892 for a recruit's widow to $7,380 for a chief-of-staff's widow. The basic entitlement is increased $29 a month for each dependent child and a widow who is housebound or in need of aid and attendants is entitled to an additional $72 a month. For dependents of veterans, compensation alone barely places widows of low ranking servicemen above the poverty threshold; however, most widows with dependent children and those over 62 years are eligible for concurrent social security benefits. Parents are eligible for support if the income of a single parent does not exceed $3,300 or $4,500 for both parents. Maximum benefits of $1,596 and $2,160, respectively, are reduced in relation to other income.

Pensions

A total of 1.0 million war veterans received $1.6 billion in disability pensions in 1976, at an average of $1,670 for the year. These pensions are paid under two separate systems. For those on pension rolls prior to July 1960, an annual pension of $945 was payable to single veterans whose income was $2,900 or less in 1976. The income limitation for veterans with one dependent was $4,200. Under this plan the veteran's net worth and his wife's earnings were not considered in computing annual income.

In 1960 Congress added a sliding scale of benefits based on the beneficiary's level of income. Veterans or their survivors who qualified for pensions prior to enactment of the 1960 law could retain the old benefits or choose to qualify under the new system which provided in 1976 a maximum annual pension of $2,076 for a single veteran and $2,232 if he had a dependent. The sliding scale of benefits operating under the 1960 law reduces the pensions paid to relatively more affluent veterans by adjusting the annuity on the basis of the recipient's other income. This system also removes the possibility that veterans with higher earnings might receive pensions yielding them less total income than those with lower earnings. For example, a single veteran with an annual income of $1,000 is entitled to a $1,728 pension, giving a combined income of $2,728. A veteran with an annual income of $1,500 receives a pension of $1,392 for a combined income of $2,892.

To qualify for a pension under the sliding scale, a veteran without dependents must earn no more than $3,300 a year, and a veteran with one dependent no more than $4,500. However, a married veteran may qualify for a pension even if his total annual family income is above the prescribed limit, because the first $1,200 of the wife's unearned income plus all of her earnings are excluded for the purposes of qualifying for a pension. Although data are not available on the amount of income received by pensioners' wives, about a quarter of the total pension benefits is paid to veterans whose spouses have some income. Home ownership is not counted as income and 10 percent of old age insurance or other public or private retirement benefits, as well as all public assistance income, are also exempt from the income limitations. A veteran cannot receive a pension if he owns considerable assets, although the precise amount has never been stated by the Veterans Administration.

Over three-fourths of pensioned veterans are also eligible to receive OASDI benefits. VA data indicate that only one in five pensioned veterans had an annual income of less than $1,000, and these veterans were entitled to a minimum annual pension of about $1,728.

Dependents of deceased veterans may also qualify for pensions. Benefits are paid to the children until they reach age 18 years or age 23 years if the beneficiary remains in school. A veteran's child is ineligible for a pension if the child's annual unearned income exceeds $2,000 or if the estate is large enough to support the child.

Altogether 1.8 million survivors received $1.2 billion in 1976, averaging $982 per family. Between 1965 and 1975 the number of widows of deceased World War II veterans who were receiving pensions nearly tripled. If recent trends continue, the number of widows of World War II veterans qualifying for pensions will rise as the mortality rate of the veterans increases and qualifying income levels are relaxed.

Since most veterans' widows with children also qualify for social security benefits, the combined potential income of veterans' survivors has significantly reduced the number of poor. Almost half of pensioned widows, however, still remained below the poverty threshold in 1975. Congress has considered restructuring the entire pension system using the Supplementary Security Income (SSI) program as a model. The proposal would provide the same minimum adequate subsistence level for both veterans and survivors. If adopted, the measure would depart from the present practice of providing special consideration to veterans and their dependents. It would instead concentrate aid on the neediest, taking into account total family income, and would provide cost of living adjustments automatically.

In contrast with the public assistance programs, veterans' benefits are administered with maximum consideration to the recipients' dignity and self-respect. Provided he can prove eligibility, the individual has only to file a simple form in order to qualify. Thereafter he is required to submit annually only the information needed by the Veterans Administration to keep his claim current and active. The annual data are filed on a simple form, supplied to the veteran or his dependent, which includes information about the veteran's assets, income, and dependents eligible to receive benefits. Once eligibility is established, the Veterans Administration makes only a cursory check on claims. Though the General Accounting Office has criticized these methods of certification, the Veterans Administration insists that the trust is justified, since spot checks made with the Internal Revenue Service in cases of questionable claims show that the incidence of false claims is small. Assistance to veterans and their surviving dependents is delivered with a maximum of respect for the recipient and a minimum of delay. The system is worthy of emulation by other public assistance programs in which onerous needs tests are made at the expense of services to the needy and at little savings to the taxpayer.

Unemployment Insurance

The objective of unemployment insurance (UI) is to provide essential aid to workers during periods of forced idleness. Unemployment insurance is not to be viewed as an antipoverty program, but as a protection earned by the worker against joblessness. Eligibility for assistance and the level of benefits are based on past earnings and work experience and not on need; so the poor are often excluded or receive inadequate benefits. The purpose of unemployment insurance is to cover nondeferrable expenditures, but without reducing the recipient's incentive to work.

Unemployment insurance was established along with the other social insurance programs under the Social Security Act of 1935. However, it was given a unique administrative structure. The law made employers in all states liable to a payroll tax; at 1975 levels the tax was 3.2 percent of the first $4,200 of an employee's annual earnings. Eighty-four percent of the taxes are returned to the states for the operation of their own programs and the rest of the funds are earmarked for the administrative costs of the program and the federal-state extended benefit program. While state programs are subject to a few federal standards, such as the extent of coverage, the states determine the duration and amount of benefits, the eligibility of the covered worker, and the amount of the employer's contribution through a system that allows reduced tax burdens for the employers who have a low unemployment experience. Therefore, it is to the employer's advantage to have state statutes that include as many barriers to qualification as possible. As a result, individual state programs vary widely even though the tax is universal. Three additional unemployment insurance programs are administered by the federal government for veterans, railroad workers, and federal government employees.

In order to establish eligibility for unemployment benefits, a worker in covered employment who finds himself out of work must meet the state's employment and earning tests, be available for work, and register with the local employment service office. Normally a weekly report of the individual's efforts to seek employment independently must be made to the employment service office.

States have additional eligibility rules that may exclude the poor from unemployment compensation. The covered worker typically must have been employed during two of the last five quarters, and most states require that earnings during the qualifying period be thirty times the weekly benefit amount, or a flat minimum sum ranging from $300 to $800 during the base period. The effect of minimum earning requirements is to force low-wage earners, who are most susceptible to unemployment, to work longer than high-wage earners in order to qualify for unemployment benefits. Also excluded are those unemployed who are just entering or reentering the labor force and those who either have been terminated for misconduct or who have left their jobs voluntarily. These and other criteria disqualify more than half of all unemployed persons at any given time.

A related problem (and one which is more significant to the poor) concerns the relationship of unemployment benefits to those who leave the labor force to enroll in manpower programs. The stipends paid to institutional training enrollees do not count toward unemployment insurance eligibility if the enrollee should have difficulty locating employment after leaving the program.

Weekly unemployment insurance benefit amounts vary widely among states. Most states compute benefits as a fraction of the worker's weekly or quarterly earnings, with maximums that are fixed amounts or fixed proportions of the state's average weekly wage; allowances are made for dependents in nine states. In fiscal 1975, maximum benefits for a claimant with no dependents ranged from $60 per week in Indiana and Illinois to $127 in the District of Columbia. Since most states had maximums higher than $80, it is clear that benefits paid to the poorest recipients are limited more by previous low personal income than by the state maximums. The working poor would be helped more by raising the percentage of the claimant's income on which benefits are paid than by boosts in maximum payments.

The duration of benefits is often as crucial to the recipient as the average weekly payment. Until recently maximum duration of payments was normally 26 weeks. As a cushion against massive unemployment experienced during the 1970s Congress extended benefits. The Extended Unemployment Compensation Act of 1970 provided that when the national seasonally-adjusted insured unemployment rate exceeded 4.5 percent for three consecutive months, the duration of benefits in all states would automatically be extended by 13 weeks. Individual states can extend benefits for a 13-week period in the same manner if their unemployment rate is above 4 percent and is equal to 120 percent of the same period a year earlier. But this proved too short as the recession deepened and the long-term unemployed exhausted their eligibility. Accordingly, the duration of benefits was temporarily lengthened to 65 weeks in 1974. These measures provided a necessary back-up system during 1976 when an estimated 4.1 million individuals exhausted regular unemployment insurance and an additional 2.8 million exhausted the additional 13 weeks eligibility. These measures, no doubt, saved many from poverty. More comprehensive protection carried a substantial price tag with total costs for fiscal 1976 estimated at $20 billion, three times the 1972 level.

More frequent and more prolonged unemployment among the poor is a significant cause of poverty. It is quite likely, then, that an increase in average benefits and their duration and of coverage under unemployment insurance programs would reduce the number of poor. The potential of unemployment benefits as an antipoverty device is limited by the fact that it *is* an insurance program. During 1974, only an estimated 10 percent of unemployment benefits were paid to the poor. As long as the amount and duration of benefits are dependent on past work experience, those in the lowliest occupations with the highest incidence of poverty will be helped the least.

Workers covered under the Social Security Act and the three separate federal unemployment compensation programs include over 85 percent of the work force. Many of the excluded workers, made up primarily of farm and domestic workers and state and local government employees, are characterized by low income and intermittent employment. The incidence of poverty also is undoubtedly greater among these groups. High unemployment rates, averaging 8.5 percent in 1975, prompted Congress to pass several emergency provisions. Among them was a temporary measure to extend coverage to unemployed domestics, farm workers, and state and local government employees. Benefits payments for up to 39 weeks until June 1976 and 26 weeks thereafter significantly increased the antipoverty impact of unemployment insurance.

WORKERS' COMPENSATION

Workers' compensation, as unemployment insurance, is designed to protect families from poverty during a period when the wages of one of its earners are reduced or interrupted due to work-connected injuries or to tide the family over if the injury is fatal. Besides cash benefits, the system also provides for medical care and rehabilitation of the injured workers.

Workers' compensation is administered in much the same manner as unemployment insurance. In each state there are separate laws and the federal government, railroad, and merchant marine operate separate programs. In 26 states during 1975, the maximum weekly benefit for a totally disabled worker was less than two-thirds the average weekly salary in the state. In 23 states the maximum payment was less than the cash income required to raise a four member family out of poverty and minimum payments were universally below the poverty standard. Although the rationale for low benefits is that they often encourage a speedy return to work, the level of benefits paid to the totally and permanently disabled and to dependent survivors is not substantially higher than that paid to temporary recipients.

Workers' compensation laws cover approximately 85 percent of the labor force. Farm and domestic workers and other low earning "casual" workers are excluded from coverage in most states. In 1975 a total of $5.1 billion was paid in benefits. Most was expended in disability compensation to injured workers, although medical and hospital care accounted for $1.8 billion in payments. An estimated eight of ten recipients of medical care are not off the job long enough to receive cash payments. However, for those requiring medical rehabilitation, the program is reported to be weak. There is no strong linkage between the federal-state vocational rehabilitation program and the workers' compensation system. Instead, vocational services received by the disabled worker are most often the result of efforts by employers and insurance carriers who have a vested interest in restoring the injured worker's productivity.

PRIVATE PENSIONS

Social security benefits alone often leave their elderly recipients near or below the poverty threshold. For a growing proportion of retirees, OASDI is supplemented by benefits from private pension or profit sharing plans which insure a more adequate standard of living. Currently, 29 million people or slightly less than half of all full-time wage and salary workers are covered by a pension or profit sharing plan. Eligibility requirements have been liberalized significantly over the last decade, increasing the proportion of covered workers ultimately qualifying for retirement benefits. By the end of 1976 it is estimated that 8.3 million beneficiaries—about one of every three retired workers—will have qualified for some private retirement benefits.

This has important ramifications for poverty among the elderly. Almost all workers covered under private plans are also covered by social security. The average private retirement benefit in 1973 was $1,920, and recipients who also qualify for social security are assured of escaping poverty in the "golden years."

Congress enacted the pension reform law in 1974 to safeguard the integrity of private pension funds and to protect the pension rights of employees who change jobs. The private retirement system is a limited antipoverty mechanism. Benefits are paid out of funds accumulated through wage deferrals and higher-paid workers are more likely to be covered. The private retirement system is a way for middle- and upper-income families to insure against poverty in old age, rather than a way for low-income workers to protect themselves for the future.

TAXING THE POOR

Along with programs providing direct income payments to the poor, several income tax provisions diminish their tax burden and can be viewed, in a sense, as indirect income payments. Tax incentives are becoming increasingly important but the benefits accruing to the poor account for a small share of the foregone revenue to the federal government.

Of importance to the poor are the additional tax exemptions for aged and blind persons and the tax exclusion of major government income transfer programs. In fiscal 1976 these measures accounted for about a tenth of the total foregone revenue:

Exclusion of social security benefits	$3.5 billion
Exclusion of unemployment insurance benefits	2.3 billion
Exclusion of public assistance benefits	.1 billion
Exclusion of veterans' benefits	.8 billion
Additional exemption for the aged and blind	1.1 billion

Although these amounts are not usually reflected in budget totals, they nonetheless provide substantial benefits to recipients.

The anomaly of the poor paying income taxes while society was trying to raise their income prompted a liberalization of the federal income tax structure. The standard deduction was raised to 16 percent of adjusted gross income and the low income allowance increased to $1,600. Deductions for personal exemptions were increased to $750 and a $30 per person tax credit was enacted. To further ease the tax burden on low income persons, provisions were made for allowing a percentage of income as a tax credit in a way that creates a limited *negative* income tax at sufficiently low income levels. The combined effect of these provisions is to exempt a worker with three dependents from paying federal income tax until his earnings exceed $6,400.

At the same time, however, other taxes on the poor remain burdensome. The social security tax of 5.85 percent is regressive, even though the upper income limit has been steadily raised. A middle-income worker pays no less than a single corporate executive with several times the salary, so the former pays a much larger share of his salary than does the latter. Nor is there any allowance for workers with large families.

State and local sales taxes also pose an increasing burden and do not exempt those on welfare or even the poorest of the poor. Many jurisdictions have sales taxes of 5 percent or more, and some jurisdictions tax food and other necessities.

Indirect taxes also take their toll through utilities bills and rent payments. In some cities, one-quarter or more of rent goes to pay for the landlord's property taxes. Aged homeowners with little income may find property taxes particularly oppressive; according to the Advisory Committee on Intergovernmental Relations, in 1970 nearly 1 million elderly homeowners with incomes below $3,000 spent more than 10 percent of their total money income on property taxes.

Overall, according to Herman P. Miller, household units with less than $4,000 annual income paid 25 percent of their total income in taxes, while units with an income between $4,000 and $25,000 paid only 30 percent—making the total tax burden only slightly progressive.

INCOME MAINTENANCE PROPOSALS

Administrative problems, the niggardliness of benefits, gaps in coverage, the rise in costs, and the continued existence of a large number of poor have led to several proposals to supplement or replace existing income maintenance programs with a more comprehensive form of cash assistance. The three basic strategies are (1) either a guaranteed income or negative income tax, (2) children's allowances, and (3) employment guarantees or wage subsidies. The first two are discussed below; public employment and minimum wage provisions are discussed in chapter 5.

Negative Income Tax

The simplest method of eliminating poverty would be to make up the income deficit of the poor in order to guarantee a minimum income. One widely discussed level is $5,500 for a family of four (in 1975 dollars). For example, a family of four with an income of $2,000 a year would receive a grant of $3,500. If the family had no income, it would receive $5,500. Such a program would require an estimated $14 billion in payments each year. However, guaranteeing a poverty-level income might reduce the pecuniary incentives to work for millions of people, since their incomes would remain at the poverty threshold whether or not they held jobs. To counter the possibility that such workers would decide to forego employment for the dole, any workable plan must allow low-wage earners to keep at least a portion of their earned income. One proposal would exempt half the earnings of low-income families in qualifying for payments. Thus a family of four with an income of $3,000 would count only $1,500 for tax purposes and be able to claim $4,000, for a total income of $6,000 compared with the $5,500 maximum paid to the family without a wage earner. Such provisions would, of course, increase the cost of the program beyond the amount needed simply to bring all poor people up to the poverty threshold. The magnitude of the cost would depend on the level of incentives offered by the plan. However, it is reasonable to estimate that the annual cost of the plan might rise to at least double the income deficit of the poor needed to bring their income to the poverty threshold. The combination of income support and earnings as proposed by President Nixon under the Family Assistance Plan is illustrated in figure 8.

The income tax structure offers the most convenient vehicle for administering such income guarantees. Though currently geared only to the collection of taxes, the reporting machinery could be adapted to distribute grants and cover income deficits—a negative income tax.

Advocates claim that the negative income tax would substitute a single, comprehensive program of income maintenance for the existing plethora of efforts. Although its simplicity is appealing, the idea does present several problems. Just as the poverty level reflects the fact that it costs more to live in a city and that AFDC payments vary from state to state, the income guarantee should adjust for cost-of-living differentials not only between urban and rural areas but also between various cities and regions. Even more basic is the determination of a family income concept and whether filing units would be altered accordingly.

The timing of payments is also important. Disbursing benefits every April 15 is obviously not often enough. However, paying monthly on the basis of the past month's earnings, for example, may not provide timely relief to a family during a particularly lean period; paying on the basis of expected earnings may introduce distortions because of inaccurate estimates. The timing of benefits and recertification of eligibility have presented problems under

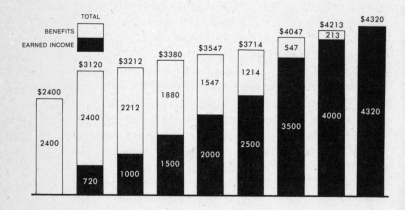

FIGURE 8

NEGATIVE INCOME TAX

WITH $2,400 GUARANTEE AND TAX RATE OF 67 PERCENT
AFTER THE FIRST $720 OF EARNINGS

AFDC and will continue to do so under a negative income tax scheme. Furthermore, some mechanism must be retained to provide assistance in emergencies.

A crucial problem in the proposed system is the selection of a base level of benefits and a "marginal tax rate," or the formula by which assistance is reduced as earnings rise. Benefits must be adequate for those who cannot provide for themselves and incentives must be attractive enough to induce the able-bodied to contribute to their own support. A low tax rate is of no help to those who cannot work, while a high benefit level may draw able-bodied workers out of the labor market. The availability of unearned benefits may decrease the earnings differential between skilled and unskilled workers and may dampen the incentive to learn skills. Combining a high benefit level with a low tax rate could qualify many middle-income families. Ever present as a constraint on benefits and incentives is the cost of such a program. Taxpayer backlash at the high costs of welfare keeps benefits low.

This tradeoff between benefits, incentives, and cost is present in any public assistance system. There is no "correct" answer, and choosing the best combination remains a question of personal values.

Family Allowances

Another method of providing cash assistance to the poor is to pay families with children a regular allowance to supplement their own incomes and meet some portion of the costs of child-rearing. This proposal recognizes that the wage system alone distributes income inadequately, because wages are based on productivity or tradition rather than on need. While the principle of equal pay for equal work is desirable as a means of eliminating discrimination based on color, age, or sex, it ignores the differing needs of families and tends to deprive children in large families of basic necessities. The underlying justification for family allowances is that a child's well-being should concern the society as a whole.

Our wage system takes little or no account of the diverse needs of workers. Except for adjustments in income taxes, for example, the take-home pay for a bachelor is the same as for the head of a

53

family with dependents in an identical job. Despite the wide acceptance of family allowances in other countries, the idea has never received active consideration in the United States—although it has been advanced on numerous occasions. AFDC is in a sense a form of family allowance, but expenditures under this program accounted for well under 1 percent of national income in 1975. A number of countries spend much more of their national income for family allowances.

Family allowances are now paid in all the industrial nations except the United States and Japan. These allowances vary widely in benefit patterns, adequacy, and financing. In some countries all children are eligible, while in others no benefits are paid for the first or second child. Benefits are usually paid for children up to the age they would normally leave school, but may be extended for further schooling, training, or apprenticeship. The allowance per child may also vary. Sweden, for examples, pays a uniform rate for all children, while France has a complex system which adjusts for family income and size and children's ages.

The adequacy of benefits ranges widely. In Canada the allowance for two children equals only 2.5 percent of the average monthly earnings in manufacturing, compared with 11 percent in Sweden. For five children, benefits varied from 6 percent in Canada to 51 percent in France. Just as benefits per child vary from country to country, so does the total magnitude of benefits. As a proportion of the gross national product, expenditures for children's allowances in 1968 ranged from less than 1 percent in West Germany, the United Kingdom, and Canada, to 1.2 percent in Sweden, and 3.6 percent in France.

Children's allowance benefits are usually financed by the national government. Many countries reinforce cash outlays with tax deductions for children. Both methods increase a family's resources for rearing children. However, Sweden eliminated the latter when it adopted the former, and the United States has only the latter.

Family allowance programs are not a complete alternative to negative income tax and are certainly no substitute for existing welfare assistance to the aged or to others without children. But because family size is so closely correlated with poverty, family allowances would lift many adults out of poverty along with their children. Family allowances have several advantages over other forms of income maintenance. There is no need for an income test, a feature that would reduce administrative costs and would maintain work incentives. Because the program gives benefits to all children, it would probably be more politically acceptable than any alternatives. The major obstacle to family allowances is the belief that, in an era when the dangers of over-population are very real, such a program would encourage procreation. This apparently has not been the case in other countries with such programs, and in any event childbearing would not be a profitable enterprise under any of the programs that have any chance of passage. Nonetheless, family allowances should be coupled with effective birth control programs to reduce the potential number of unwanted children.

Pending Welfare Proposals

Reflecting dissatisfaction with current operations of the welfare system, a number of alternatives have been proposed and debated in recent years. The debates thus far have resulted in little action. Nonetheless, a few vital issues have emerged: the level of assistance, incentives, and requirements to work, and the overlap with in-kind benefits.

Most of the suggestions covered all families with children, thus adding to AFDC families the "working poor" but not the poor without children. However, one proposal would have added a "demogrant," or payment to each person, regardless of family status. Instead of the fragmented AFDC program in which each state operated independently but with federal contributions, the federal government would establish a uniform minimum nationwide benefit schedule. Proposed benefit levels ranged from half of the poverty threshold to 50 percent above it. The lower level of support would have constituted an increase over AFDC payments in only a few states. However, the states would not be prevented from supplementing the federal payments. The maximum proposal would have included a broad chunk of the populace and would have been extremely expensive. In some versions the payment was solely a transfer, but in other proposals public service jobs would be available at low rates of pay to supplement low base payments.

Determining who was employable and whether employable family members should be encouraged or required to work was another stumbling block. The most lenient proposals included no coercion, allowing welfare mothers to choose whether to stay home with their children or go to work, and offered attractive incentives to work, permitting recipients to keep up to two-thirds of their earnings. Others envisioned harsh requirements that recipients find employment, take make-work jobs, or undergo training, and included paltry work incentives of as little as one-third of earnings.

Meshing cash assistance with existing in-kind programs presented two thorny problems. First, each program provided that benefits be reduced as earnings increased. These reductions, however, were not coordinated, so the cumulative "marginal tax rates" for the several programs sometimes approached or even exceeded 100 percent. This meant that recipients *lost* economic benefits by working more. Second, some variations disqualified recipients of cash relief from obtaining certain in-kind benefits. The increased cash, it was argued, would more than substitute for the loss of food stamps. But this was not always true. Not only would some families gain only a few dollars to compensate for the loss of several hundred dollars in in-kind benefits, but other families, in states paying more than the federal minimum, would lose the in-kind aid and receive nothing at all in return.

The rapid growth of food stamps, Medicaid, supplemental security income, and unemployment benefits has diminished the prospects of a guaranteed income. The evolution of a comprehensive benefit system, though not uniform, has increased the number of variables to be considered in reform.

Depending on the coverage, benefit levels, work incentives, and other factors, these proposals ranged in cost from a few billion dollars to nearly $100 billion. A debate with so many combatants and so many issues could result in legislation only after considerable political compromise. Of particular significance is the fact that income maintenance was recognized as a federal responsibility and that a guaranteed income for at least part of the population was a viable political issue. The failure to reach a compromise indicated that the poor had little clout and that conflicting interests among the poor dissipated whatever power they possessed.

ADDITIONAL READINGS

Barth, Michael C.; Carcagno, George J.; and Palmer, John L. *Toward An Effective Income Support System: Problems, Prospects, and Choices.* Madison, Wisc.: Institute for Research on Poverty, 1974.

Booth, Philip. *Social Security in America.* Ann Arbor, Mich.: University of Michigan, Institute of Labor and Industrial Relations, 1973.

Levitan, Sar A.; Rein, Martin; and Marwick, David. *Work and Welfare Go Together.* Baltimore: The Johns Hopkins University Press, 1976.

Levitan, Sar A. and Alderman, Karen Cleary. *Old Wars Remain Unfinished: The Veteran Benefits System.* Baltimore: The Johns Hopkins University Press, 1973 and 1975 supplement.

Pechman, Joseph A. and Timpane, P. Michael (eds.). *Work Incentives and Income Guarantees.* Washington: The Brookings Institution, 1975.

Steiner, Gilbert Y. *The State of Welfare.* Washington: The Brookings Institution, 1971.

Unemployment Compensation Amendments: Legislative Analysis. Washington: American Enterprise Institute for Public Policy Research, 1976.

3

Provision of Services and Goods

For I was hungry and you gave me food, I was thirsty and you gave me
  drink, I was a stranger and you welcomed me,
I was naked and you clothed me, I was sick and you visited me, I was
  in prison and you came to me.

—Matthew 25:35–36

In our society the state has assumed the responsibility for providing many goods and services to its citizens. Most of these benefits
are dispensed without regard to the recipients' level of income, and
cost far more than all programs expressly designed for the poor.
For example, educating the nation's children and youth costs all
levels of government twice as much as do outlays aimed directly at
aiding the poor. Beyond the direct public services is what the late
Richard M. Titmuss called the "iceberg phenomenon of social
welfare." This refers to the revenue system that exempts certain
types of expenditures from income taxes. One of the quite numerous examples of this "fiscal welfare" system is the provision allowing home owners to deduct interest paid on home mortgages from
regular income subject to taxation. It must be noted that many
direct public services—as well as the "fiscal welfare" provisions—
tend to favor the affluent members of society over the poor. An
authoritative foreign observer of the American scene, Gunnar
Myrdal, has observed, "In almost all respects . . . American eco-

58

nomic and social policies show a perverse tendency to favor groups that are above the level of the most needy."

This chapter is concerned primarily with the goods and services that the government makes available on the basis of need. Provided are both necessities—such as medical care, food, and shelter —and various services which are designed to improve the "quality of life" of the poor.

These goods and services are provided either directly by the government or by others who are in turn paid by the government. Compensatory education is provided by the government directly to the poor. Most health care for the poor, on the other hand, is provided indirectly, with all three levels of government sharing the costs. In covering the cost of specific goods and services, such payments differ from general income supplements but allow more freedom of choice than the direct provision of necessities. Poor people can select their own physicians rather than depend on the care available in public institutions.

In-kind assistance has grown rapidly and accounted for three-fifths of total outlays per poor person in 1974 compared to one-fifth of outlays one decade earlier (figure 9).

MEDICAL SERVICES

The linkage between poverty and poor health has long been recognized, and medical services are now considered by our society as an essential ingredient of even a minimum standard of living. Since the passage of Medicare and Medicaid in 1965, the federal government has assumed the major responsibility as provider of the health care for the aged and the poor. The estimated 1974 federal contribution to health care programs in aid of the poor amounted to more than $6.4 billion (table 3).

Despite these massive public expenditures, the deficit in health care to the poor remains startling, whether measured in life expectancy, infant mortality rate, or numbers of visits to physicians or dentists. Considering the expanding government outlays, what accounts for the deficiencies in health care? No doubt some of the funds are wasted by inept administration; and as in other areas,

59

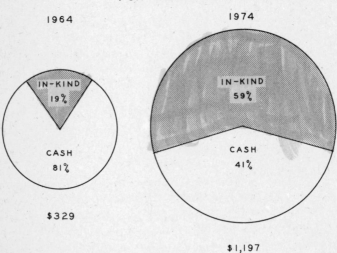

FIGURE 9
PER CAPITA CASH AND IN-KIND ASSISTANCE
FOR THE POOR

1964

1974

IN-KIND
19%

CASH
81%

IN-KIND
59%

CASH
41%

$329

$1,197

Source: U.S. Office of Management and Budget

Table 3. Federal outlays for medical care to the poor, 1974

Program	(millions)
Total	*$6,389*
Medicare	1,928
Medicaid	3,138
Community Health Projects	500
Veterans	298
Maternal and Child Health	301
Indians	141
Other	84

SOURCE: U.S. Department of Health, Education, and Welfare

the poor pay more, especially when the government foots the bill. Waste and overcharges account only partially for the soaring medical costs. The following salient factors explain the persisting health deficiencies of the poor:

1. The poor, on the average, need more medical attention because of the greater proportion of aged persons among them, and because of the physical and mental handicaps most frequently associated with poverty.

2. The poor are offered little preventive medical attention. Federal funds for health care of children are extremely limited, and the health care that is available only encourages delay in correcting health problems or defects until they become major problems.

3. The delivery of existing health services, which is generally inefficient, is particularly disorganized when applied to the poor; community health services are fragmented and often inaccessible. Shortages of medical and allied manpower have retarded the establishment of adequate health services in neighborhoods where economic incentives are limited.

Medicare and Medicaid

The federal government's most important health care programs are Medicare and Medicaid, both added to the Social Security Act in 1965. Medicare covers the bulk of hospital and medical costs of persons who are 65 years of age and older and, as of 1973, persons who are disabled social security beneficiaries. All social se-

90 days

curity and railroad retirement recipients and others who meet special qualifications are entitled to hospital insurance (HI). In 1976, 24.3 million persons were covered, and about 5.7 million received hospital care. HI pays a major part of the costs of up to 90 days of hospitalization, as well as post-hospital extended care and home health services.

All persons entitled to HI benefits, as well as retired federal employees, are also eligible for supplementary medical insurance (SMI). This plan helps pay the cost of doctors' and surgeons' fees, diagnostic tests, medical supplies, and prescription drugs.

$8.00

In 1976 about 13.2 million persons—over half of those eligible —were served. The enrollee pays a ~~$6.70~~ monthly premium that is matched by the federal government. Individuals enrolled in the program also pay a $60 deductible per year before receipt of benefits and 20 percent of costs in addition to the deductible amount, bringing the recipient's out-of-pocket costs to $140 per year before SMI contributions become available. The plan's premium costs discourage many aged near-poor from purchasing SMI. States are required to pay premiums, deductibles, and the 20 percent of uncovered costs for the elderly people receiving supplementary security income payments. People who are "medically needy"—those whose income is barely above the poverty threshold—must pay their own premiums, although states may pay deductibles and additional out-of-pocket costs. However, only nine states and the District of Columbia provide these benefits for their elderly medically needy population.

An Office of Economic Opportunity report estimated that one-fourth of Medicare outlays aid the poor in obtaining medical care. No doubt the program has kept others out of poverty and eased the anxieties of those whose life savings would have been wiped out as the result of illness.

The medical assistance program (Medicaid) is more significant for the poor. Persons receiving federally supported public assistance in all states except Arizona are eligible, and 29 states and the District of Columbia extend eligibility to persons who do not qualify for public assistance but whose income is sufficiently low to qualify them as "medically needy." In 1976 the federal contribution to the payment of medical services to nearly 23.2 million persons via Medicaid amounted to $8.2 billion, three-fourths of which aided persons below the poverty threshold. Despite Medicare benefits, persons over 65 years of age require the largest portion of Medicaid funds (figure 10).

Medicaid was designed to replace the separate medical assistance plans of the four public assistance programs. It contributes to the medical costs of recipients, the federal share ranging from 50 to 83 percent, depending upon the scope of services and eligibility requirements. The states set most of the rules but are subject to some federal regulation. In 1968 Congress restricted Medicaid to families with an income of no more than a third above the AFDC income cut-off—a step taken because several states had set significantly higher income ceilings. Ceilings ranged in 1974 from $1,400 to $2,200 for individuals and from $2,700 to $5,600 for a family of four.

In an attempt to improve the quality of medical services, the government has also required states to set standards for hospitals and physicians to help attract well-qualified physicians by reimbursing them at prevailing local rates. To allay fears of "socialized medicine," no provision was made for federal monitoring, however, and Medicaid has been racked by disclosures of unconscionable charges by some physicians ministering to the health needs of the poor. Studies have revealed cases of physicians who claimed reimbursement for 150 welfare patients in a single day.

Congress sought to remedy such unethical behavior and to tighten the law requiring the payment of "reasonable cost" by directing HEW to spell out standards controlling the reimbursement of hospitals and physicians under Medicare, Medicaid, and maternal and child health programs. Self-regulation remained virtually in effect, leaving the administration of Medicaid and other federal health care programs loosely monitored, until concern over abuse of federal health programs resulted in congressionally-mandated institution of professional standards review organizations in 1972 representing local practitioners to monitor Medicare and Medicaid services. As of 1976 the system of review boards was not fully implemented.

FIGURE 10
MEDICAID 1975

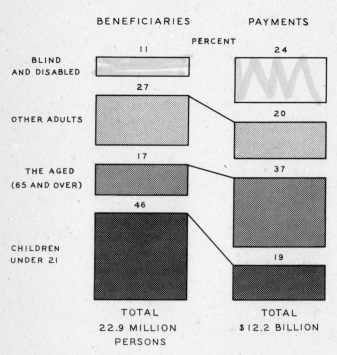

BENEFICIARIES   PAYMENTS

PERCENT

	BENEFICIARIES	PAYMENTS
BLIND AND DISABLED	11	24
OTHER ADULTS	27	20
THE AGED (65 AND OVER)	17	37
CHILDREN UNDER 21	46	19

TOTAL   TOTAL
22.9 MILLION $12.2 BILLION
PERSONS

Source: U.S. Department of Health, Education, and Welfare

Community Health Projects

Given the expansion of federal outlays for the health care of the poor, the challenge of improving medical care and the efficiency of the health industry in delivering services to the poor became paramount. It was inevitable that programs initiated under the Economic Opportunity Act would experiment with the means to accomplish this end. Perhaps the most important efforts were the neighborhood health centers established by the Office of Economic Opportunity. Compared with other government contributions to medical services for the poor, the outlays for health centers were no more than a proverbial drop in the bucket. Assuming that improving the health of the poor required not only massive funds but also major changes in the health care delivery system, the antipoverty agency undertook to establish centers which embraced four elements (1) a full range of ambulatory health services, (2) close liaison with other community services, (3) close working relationships with a hospital (preferably one with medical school affiliation), and (4) participation of the indigenous population in decisionmaking and employment in the centers.

Support of the centers continued under HEW auspices after the dismantling of the antipoverty agency. In 1976 HEW contributed to a total of 234 community health centers including 77 rural health projects. Federal support for these projects amounted to $201 million in 1975.

Veterans

A variety of other programs provide subsidized health care for the poor, most of them concentrating on specific groups, i.e., Indians, veterans, migrants, or handicapped children. The most important of these is the medical program for veterans.

The Veterans Administration health care system, originally designed to care for war wounded, currently provides free care on a broad scale to aged and indigent veterans whose medical needs are in no way related to military service.

The VA expended $3.8 billion on medical care in 1976. The system operates 172 hospitals, 89 nursing care units, 18 domiciliaries, and 229 outpatient clinics. Also the VA contributes to the cost of care received by veterans in state-run domiciliaries and nursing homes. All "medically indigent" war veterans are eligible for VA hospital care, and most of the patients in VA hospitals have no service-connected injury. The criteria for eligibility are based not on set income limitations, but on the individual's opinion of what he can afford. Although access to the veterans health care system does not demand poverty as an eligibility criterion, many of the patients using veterans' hospitals are poor. The system, in fact, saves many individuals from economic disaster when costly illness strikes.

Indians

The American Indian living on a reservation and the Alaskan native are perhaps the most poverty stricken minorities in the country. About three-fifths of American Indians live on isolated reservations. Native Alaskans tend to be inland village dwellers. Neither of these geographic or economic settings attracts private establishment of health facilities. Although native Americans are eligible for Medicaid, about one-fourth of the reservation population resides in Arizona, the only state without Medicaid programs. Poor roads and inadequate transportation and communication limit access to outlying care facilities, especially when the individual is hampered by illness. Isolation and poverty take their tolls. Indians have the nation's highest incidence of tuberculosis and suffer disproportionately from streptococcal infections, nutritional and dental deficiencies, poor mental health, and attendant disorders.

The Indian Health Service in HEW helps provide medical needs, employing 8,500 health care personnel in 51 federally-operated hospitals and 91 outpatient clinics located on or near reservations. Contracted services are also acquired in nonfederal facilities. The purchase of care for over 109,000 hospital admissions, 2.8 million visits to outpatient and mental health clinics, visiting health workers services, and facility construction and renovation accounted for the $280 million expenditure by the Indian Health Service in 1976.

The Indian Health Service's efforts, which have been vastly expanded in the preceding decades, are now paying off. Between 1960 and 1974 the life expectancy of Indians increased 2.9 years. The Indian death rate from influenza and pneumonia decreased 70 percent. The infant mortality rate has dropped from 50 to 19 deaths per 1,000 live births. Family planning services are rendered to more than one-fourth the female population between 15 and 44 years of age and, consequently, the birth rate per 1,000 population has dropped from 43 births to 31 births. There has been a decline in the number of new tuberculosis cases and the deaths caused by that disease.

Progress in lessening the tremendous health deficit of Indians has been considerable. However, compared with the rest of the population it is evident that the Indian Health Service has conquered a mole hill on top of a mountain. Facilities remain primitive compared with sophisticated city hospitals, and the service lacks adequate and experienced personnel. Without the draft, doctors who had fulfilled their military requirement by working on reservations will no longer be available. Turnover of other personnel contributes to the persisting cultural gaps between the health workers and the target population. More extensive training of Indian health personnel would help alleviate these deficiencies and create a health manpower pool with roots in the community. In order to improve the health of the native American population, underlying deficiencies in housing, nutrition, and health education must also be corrected.

SHELTER

On the average, 15 percent of consumer expenditures are for rent or home ownership costs and 7 percent more are for furnishings and equipment. Given the high and rising prices of shelter, both old and new, poor families are faced with grim choices: they can live in substandard units, they can economize on space by crowding into dwellings which are more adequate, or they can use a disproportionate share of their meager incomes for housing. In many cases, they must resort to all three. Out of the 76 million

67

unit, year-round housing stock in 1974, 2.1 million units lacked plumbing facilities, and an indeterminate number were dilapidated and in need of major repair. In the same year, there were 3.4 million occupied units with more than one person per room—the accepted American standard for overcrowding. Four of 10 renter families had to spend more than a fourth of their income for shelter and utilities.

Federal policies have contributed significantly to the alleviation of the nation's housing problems. The broader approach has been to promote the construction of new homes for middle-income families, hopefully opening vacancies for lower-income renters and home buyers. Roughly 23 percent of all mortgage loans for private homes in 1975 were guaranteed by the Federal Housing Administration, the Veterans Administration, or the Farmers Home Administration. Savings to homeowners and rental property owners from special tax treatment amounted to about $10 billion. All these forms of assistance stimulate housing construction, and though the poor receive only a minute proportion of this aid, they may benefit from the "trickle-down" effect. The 80 percent decline in substandard housing between 1960 and 1974 and the 30 percent increase in housing over the same period of time were in part the result of federal incentives and aids for new construction.

Of more direct importance to the poor, however, are the various federal programs that subsidize the building, rental, leasing, purchase, and operation of apartments and houses for low-income households. At the end of fiscal 1975, there were 2.9 million units available for occupancy involving an annual subsidy of about $2.0 billion (table 4). Two-thirds of these units had been produced since 1968.

The oldest and largest housing assistance program to the poor is public housing. Initiated in 1937, the public housing program provides federal subsidies for the amortization of construction costs on units built, owned, and operated by local housing authorities. The units are reserved for low-income families, with locally established income limits, usually less than $3,500 for a family of three. With the federal subsidy to cover capital costs, rents need to cover only the operating expense; typically, they are between one-half

Table 4. Federally subsidized housing units, completed or under management as of June 30, 1975

	(in thousands)
Total	2,890
Public housing including leased	1,151
Rent Supplement (excluding Section 236 units)	103
Interest rate subsidies for home ownership (235)	409
Interest rate subsidies for rentals (236)	400
Elderly	42
Rehabilitation loans and grants	113
Farmers Home Administration programs	672

SOURCE: U.S. Departments of Housing and Urban Development and Agriculture.

and one-third less than market rates for similar units. Some of the poor are unable to pay even this low rent without using more than a fourth of their adjusted incomes. Since 1969, the federal government has been authorized to make up the difference between operating costs and what tenants can reasonably pay, in addition to the capital amortization subsidy.

Building and operating housing for low-income families is a massive undertaking that can get very expensive. In 1975 there were 1,151,000 units operated at an annual subsidy of about $850 per unit, not including an operating subsidy of an additional $400 per unit. By the end of fiscal year 1977, 294,000 more units are expected to be ready for occupancy and a total of more than 800,000 units are expected to be approved for construction or rehabilitation. Public housing is serving the purpose for which it was designed. Of the families that moved in or were reexamined for continued occupancy in the year ending September 30, 1975, nearly three-quarters were receiving some kind of low-income assistance or benefits. More than two-thirds of the families had no one working. A quarter to a third of the families were headed by an elderly person. The median income for all the families was about $3,350 and they paid a median annual rent of $660.

Public housing has been plagued by a number of difficulties. To save costs and to avoid opposition, many public housing units have been located in large-scale, inner-city projects. Concentrating poor families and locating them in deteriorating neighborhoods has led to problems of vandalism, crime, and general malaise among tenants. Plagued by the shortage of funds, many central city housing authorities had no choice but to let their units deteriorate. The additional operating subsidies provided by Congress in 1970 saved some local housing authorities from collapse, but were inadequate to accomplish all needed improvements. In many areas, public housing is still far short of a "decent home and suitable living environment," though it is still better than alternatives, as long waiting lists attest.

To overcome the problems of public housing, several new approaches were tried in the 1960s and 1970s. To encourage the dispersal of low-income families throughout the community, the Housing and Urban Development Act of 1964 provided subsidies to local authorities to lease privately-owned units for eligible families who would then pay public housing rentals. But most of the 400,000 units leased by 1976 differed little from public housing projects in that there was little progress in penetrating more affluent neighborhoods. A 1976 Supreme Court decision held that HUD could be ordered to correct housing segregation by extending remedial measures beyond city limits into suburban areas. However unless there is an interest on the part of the suburbs for expanding housing opportunities for the poor, the effect of the ruling may be minimal.

A rent supplement program, initiated in 1965, subsidized the rent paid by low-income families living in designated privately-owned units. The subsidy makes up the difference between the market rents and one-fourth of the tenant's adjusted income. The hope, as under leasing, was that low-income families could be dispersed and that rent subsidized units could be sprinkled among nonsubsidized housing. In fact, however, most of the 69,000 units at the end of fiscal 1972 were either in completely rent supplemented projects, or used in tandem with other subsidy programs to reach an even lower income clientele.

The Housing and Urban Development Act of 1968 added two more subsidy programs which became for a while the primary focus of activity. One approach known as the "236" program (corresponding to the appropriate section of the act) provides subsidies to lenders so that the interest rate on privately-owned low-income rental housing projects can be reduced to 1 percent.

However, since the rents must cover the operating costs plus capital repayment costs, the rents are higher and the tenants must have a higher income level. To offset the higher rents built into the 236 program, many of the units are also covered by the rent supplement program. In 1975 a little more than 400,000 units were assisted by the 236 program, with 62,000 of them receiving rent supplements. The median annual income of those who moved in during 1975 was $5,634, $2,280 higher than for public housing tenants. More than two-thirds of the families had at least one person working. Only 11 percent were headed by elderly persons.

The 235 homeownership program seeks to help lower-income families become property owners by requiring lower down payments and interest rate subsidies to hold down the cost of mortgage payments. However because few families below the poverty level can afford capital repayments, upkeep, and taxes, this program benefits the near-poor more than those in poverty. Only 5 percent of the 323,000 buyers who bought homes during the first four years of the program had an annual income of less than $4,000. The number of units covered by the program reached a peak of 419,000 in 1974 after the Nixon administration terminated new commitments under the program. In 1975, 10,000 fewer units were covered by the program.

Although the housing programs have assuredly succeeded in making some decent housing affordable to the poor, the overall record was not without serious flaws. The objective of dispersing subsidized housing out of concentrated pockets in urban centers has not been met. Local resistance to spreading low-cost housing and piggybacked programs has limited the reach of the programs to smaller areas and fewer persons than would probably be possible otherwise. The unexpectedly large and growing commitment for operating subsidies mandates alternative solutions for the long run.

As a partial consequence of the problems and failures of the national housing program, in January 1973 the Nixon administration put an 18 month moratorium on all new authorizations of subsidized housing starts. While projects in process were allowed to continue, the intent was to hold up any new commitments until housing assistance programs and strategies could be reevaluated and redesigned. Federal housing assistance efforts got back on track in mid-1974 with the passage of the Housing and Community Development Act of 1974. The act cut back the strong federal role in establishing a national housing policy by directing more than three quarters of the total authorization into a program of community block grants to be spent according to broad guidelines. The act also authorized a new rental assistance program and conventional public housing construction, in addition to assistance for the elderly. The home ownership program and the rental program were authorized to continue temporarily on a reduced basis, but in fact are being terminated. In an effort to relieve some of the nonproductive maintenance expenses for upkeep of vacant federally-owned housing units, the act authorized HUD to transfer to local housing authorities small (1–4 units) residential dwellings. They are sold at nominal cost to poor or near-poor persons under an urban homesteading program.

Aside from assuming a direct financial burden, Congress has taken legislative action beyond the open housing laws to get to the cause of some of the urban housing problems. Hoping to increase the private resources available for mortgages on inner city homes, Congress, in 1975, passed legislation to discourage "redlining" by private lenders. "Redlining," the practice of marking out certain urban areas and refusing to make loans in the areas regardless of personal credit-worthiness, has been singled out as a major factor in central city decay. The new law does not prohibit the practice but instead forces lending institutions to disclose the amount of mortgage money they lend to different areas of a city. The theory is that depositors and bank customers will not patronize banks that shut off mortgages to certain areas of a city. Whether the law works that way remains to be seen. The legislation is an important attempt to place the initiative for action into the private market.

The federal government still is committed to supporting construction of lower income housing and subsidizing and underwriting interest costs for private construction for low-income tenants. But the emphasis in housing—as in other social action areas—is on returning the strategy initiative to the market and down to the local level. Whether community officials can make good use of the federal dollar remains to be seen.

FOOD

Federal food expenditures ballooned from less than $1 billion in 1968 to about $8 billion in fiscal 1976. This rapid growth reflects broad support for providing food directly to the poor instead of allocating a portion of their cash assistance to food. Some saw food programs as a way of getting more for the poor by raising the cry of "hunger in America." Others favored food distribution because they were concerned that the poor would use their cash grants unwisely. And still others sought to sustain the demand for certain agricultural products. A number of programs were developed, with varying eligibility requirements and types of aid offered. More than 90 percent of the benefits under these programs are distributed on the basis of need, and the poor receive most of the help; the balance is not income-conditioned, and the poor also benefit from these programs (figure 11).

Food Stamps

By far the largest food subsidy program is the food stamp program, which increases the purchasing power of about 19 million persons at a cost of about $5.6 billion annually. Under this plan, eligible persons and families may exchange money they would normally spend on food for coupons whose value is greater than the amount paid. The coupons may then be exchanged in retail stores for food. A monthly coupon allotment is set for each household size, and the value of the bonus decreases as income rises. The very poorest families receive the food stamps free, and others are supposed to pay no more than 30 percent of their income. The food allotment for a family of four in 1975 was $154 and the subsidy ranged from 100 percent for a family with an income under $30 per month to 26 percent (payment of $130) for a

73

FIGURE II
FOOD ASSISTANCE
1972 AND 1976

CHILD NUTRITION
$2.3 BILLION

CHILD NUTRITION
$1.3 BILLION

COMMODITIES
$.3 BILLION

FOOD STAMPS
$5.6 BILLION

FOOD STAMPS
$1.9 BILLION

1972   1976

Source: U.S. Office of Management and Budget

family with a monthly income of $510. Overall, recipients double the value of their food dollars. All public assistance recipients are eligible, as are other households living in poverty. An estimated three-fifths of all food stamp recipients in 1973 were also cash welfare recipients, and 36 percent also received social security.

The federal food stamp program, in operation nationally from 1939 to 1943, was revived in 1961 and is available in all states. After a slow start in the 1960s the program expanded rapidly during the 1970s.

Fiscal	Participants (millions)	Costs (billions)
1969	2.9	$ .2
1971	9.4	1.6
1973	12.2	2.2
1975	14.0	4.7
1976	19.0	5.6

Although recipients would undoubtedly find cash easier and less demeaning to use, food stamps may be used to purchase any food for human consumption except alcoholic beverages, tobacco, and imported food (no Russian caviar). Aside from the fact that food stamps cannot be used for housecleaning and laundry supplies, medicines, and many other items carried in supermarkets, there are other operational limitations. The household must purchase the full amount of coupons at the beginning of each month, often leaving little cash for anything else, even in an emergency. Nor are benefits adequate. The food stamp bonus is supposed to enable a family to maintain what the Department of Agriculture calls a "nutritionally adequate" diet, but this regimen requires nutritional planning skills, storage space, equipment, and low-cost markets.

In an attempt to restrict food stamps only to those who could not support themselves, Congress established a work requirement. Except for persons with child-care responsibilities, students, and persons already working, all able-bodied persons between 18 and 65 in households receiving food stamps must register for employment and accept suitable work paying the going rate in the locality, even though that may be below the federal minimum in some cases. Finally, program administration has been criticized because eligibility and benefits for food stamps and for cash assistance are often maintained separately and because outlets for purchasing food stamps are often distant from beneficiaries and are typically understaffed, requiring long waiting.

The rapid growth of food stamps in the early 1970s paralleled the growth of cash welfare in the late 1960s. Among the important factors were:

1. the wider availability of benefits. About 60 percent of the population in 1969 lived in areas served by the program; by 1975 all of the population had access to food stamp benefits, as the commodity distribution program was phased out.

2. more generous benefits. Congress enacted higher benefits generally and provided that the poorest families should get food stamps free. In addition, benefits are to be adjusted semi-annually by the increase in the cost-of-living.

3. an increasing proportion of public assistance households, who are automatically eligible, availed themselves of benefits.

4. higher unemployment during the 1970s. The Agriculture Department estimated in 1975 that each 1 percent rise in the unemployment rate might add about 600,000 additional participants.

5. wider knowledge. Additional persons were prompted to apply for benefits because of extensive media publicity and the outreach efforts of public and private groups.

A purported reason cited by the program's critics was fraud. Although there were many errors in determining eligibility and computing benefits, these errors had a limited effect on the overall number of recipients, and charges of widespread fraud were not substantiated. In spite of the extensive and rapid growth, it was estimated that for every person receiving benefits in 1975, another eligible person was not receiving benefits.

The program is fairly successful in targeting benefits to those most in need and in offering assistance to the working poor. According to Agriculture Department estimates, a quarter of participating households had an income of less than $2,000, another 50 percent were between $2,000 and $5,000, and virtually no families had an income of $10,000 or more. Put another way, seven of every ten American families with incomes under $2,000 were participants, as were 40 percent of all families with an income below $5,000. Some families who would not normally be considered poor were able to participate because various costs were deducted from a family's gross income to compute eligibility and benefit amount. Included in the deductibles were federal, state, and local taxes and certain shelter, medical care, education, child care, and work expenses. It was estimated that an average household had a gross cash income of $2,856 a year plus deductions totaling $672, leaving a net income for food stamp purposes of $182 a month. It was estimated that this average family had additional in-kind income of $126 a month.

An analysis of recipient characteristics showed that about one of three recipient households was headed by a male. Nearly half of the family heads were 55 years or older and over half of all participants were 18 years or younger.

Concerned by the increase in beneficiaries and potential further expansion, the administration moved in mid-1976 to substantially restrict eligibility and reduce benefit levels for the near-poor while increasing levels of support for the more needy. The administration proposed limited eligibility for food stamps to families with an annual income of $1,200 above the poverty threshold ($1,500 if a household member is over 65 years old). About 5 million persons benefiting from food stamps would have become ineligible under the new regulations. The food subsidy was set at 30 percent of income above the standard deduction level. For example, a family of 4 with an annual income of $4,000 was entitled to a maximum food subsidy of $1,152 (maximum annual food subsidy of $1,992 less 30 percent of $2,800).

Child Nutrition

A variety of child nutrition programs provide breakfasts, lunches, and milk to children in public and private schools and day care centers, at a total federal cost in fiscal 1976 of about $2.3 billion. By far the largest is the school lunch program, with federal costs in fiscal 1976 of about a billion dollars. Nearly 27 million children, about five of every nine, received lunch daily. Federal reimbursement is provided on the basis of all meals served, regardless of children's family income, and additional assistance is provided for meals served free or at reduced cost to children from poor or near-poor families. Required state matching contributions and children's payments amounted to over $2 billion. In the 1975–76 school year about 10.6 million children received free meals at an average federal subsidy of 79 cents per meal; and 15.1 million children received lunches at an average federal cost of 23 cents. In addition, the federal government expended about $150 million for breakfasts served to 2.4 million school children, most of whom were from poor families. Over $100 million is spent on a summer food program designed to reach some 3 million school-age children. Institutions where one-third of the children are needy qualified for the program, and free meals were served to all children.

Preschool children received year-round food assistance in child-care centers, including food service programs in Head Start centers. Almost 600,000 children, mostly from poor families, received these meals free. Finally, some $432 million worth of commodities were provided in fiscal 1975 to schools and child-care institutions.

Despite the significant progress, some serious flaws remain in the school lunch program, especially in serving the poor. For every two children who received free or reduced-price lunches, at least one more child, perhaps several million altogether, was eligible but did not benefit. The process of establishing eligibility can be complicated for the applicant and can create a great deal of paper work for the schools. Moreover, children who qualify for free or reduced-price lunches are often singled out by standing in separate lines, eating at specified tables, or using distinctive lunch tokens. The involved certification procedures and stigmatization of children may discourage many needy children from applying for free meals. Many more children are denied this opportunity because their school does not have the necessary equipment or funds to meet federal matching requirements for operating expenses. This is especially true of schools in poor neighborhoods. Thus, those children who most need the nutritional benefits of a school lunch are also those most likely to go to schools without such programs.

SOCIAL SERVICES

The poor need more than income. In addition to food, shelter, and medical programs which supplement their cash income, a variety of social services are available to assist the poor. Social services include such diverse activities that they defy definition. Their scope can be indicated, however, by a catalog of illustrative activities or broad social objectives. [They range from specifics, such as legal aid or family planning, to the more vague forms of assistance, such as counseling or strengthening family life. The mere process of determining whether someone has a problem, even if nothing can be done to relieve it, is regarded as a social service.]

If the content of social services is amorphous, the cost is not. Starting in 1967 open-ended federal matching funds (three federal dollars for every state dollar) were available to finance a wide variety of services for former, current, or potential welfare recipients. Concerned because state requests for these funds quickly ballooned to over $4 billion, Congress imposed an annual $2.5 billion ceiling on federal expenditures for this purpose in 1972. The same law raised federal matching funds to 90 percent for family planning services.

Disputes over 1973 regulation proposals that would have severely restricted state discretion in charging federal social service dollars prompted additional legislation. A 1974 law, which confined social service expenditures to more specific goals, directed that at least half of expenditures aid public assistance recipients and restricted free services to families whose income was below the national median or 80 percent of the state median income.

Child-care funding accounted for one-fourth of the $2.95 billion expended on social services in 1976, including 77 percent federal dollars. Other large components included foster care, services to the mentally retarded, drug and alcohol abuse treatment, and family planning programs.

COMMUNITY ACTION

The impact of most antipoverty programs is ultimately constrained because of the insulated bureaucracy administering them.

With program operators far removed from the program clients, help is frequently offered grudgingly and with scant regard for the recipients' self esteem. Sensitive to these problems, the Great Society's antipoverty architects sought a strategy for fighting poverty that required participation by the poor in the design and operation of the programs. They attempted to involve the poor in the decisionmaking process, determining which services would be responsive and how they were supposed to be delivered. The general approach was to involve the poor to permit as much discretion and encourage as much innovation as possible at the local level. Three principle vehicles for this new approach were the Community Action Program (CAP), legal services, and the community development corporations.

A product of the Great Society's 1964 Economic Opportunity Act, CAP funded the establishment of almost 1,000 local community action agencies (CAA) in urban neighborhoods, in rural areas, and on Indian reservations. The poor were represented on their planning boards and in many cases were hired to help operate the programs. This experience better equipped the poor to work in solving their own problems. Although the 1967 amendments to the Economic Opportunity Act (EOA) sought to bring more CAAs under public control, only 140 (about half of these were Indian CAPs) were public before President Nixon urged the withdrawal of federal assistance to CAAs. Congress agreed to terminate the Office of Economic Opportunity as a separate agency but extended support to CAAs under the Community Services Administration, a newly established bureau in the Department of Health, Education, and Welfare.

The CAAs have been a catchall for projects to aid the poor and they act as sponsors for a variety of social programs funded by federal, state, local, and private agencies. Practically any effort aimed at reducing poverty may be funded through CAAs. However, the moves to consolidate manpower spending and encourage comprehensive manpower planning at the local level hurt the CAAs. The Comprehensive Employment and Training Act of 1973 designated elected officials, not CAAs, as prime sponsors for federally funded employment and training programs. The act also limited direct participation by the poor in the planning and policy formulation stage to an advisory status. In spite of the loss of power and in some cases, the loss of some funds, nearly 900 CAAs are still active in manpower programs, as well as in a multitude of other social programs providing services at the local level directly to the poor.

The long-run CAP strategy was to mobilize nonfederal resources to respond to local needs. Changes in local public and private institutions are being effected by giving the poor the tools to make their needs known to local government officials, civil organizations, employers, and labor interests who are in the position to give direct help to the poor in the community. These improvements are encouraging. But the strength of any commitment between local and private institutions and the poor is only now being tested. Rampant inflation and the 1974–75 recession have left many local governments on the brink of insolvency and eager to cut costs wherever possible. In fiscal 1977 the federal share for CAAs will be down to 60 percent. Whether the CAAs and the poor persons they represent can continue to command the local support that is becoming increasingly vital to them, remains to be seen.

Closely related to the CAAs is VISTA (Volunteers in Service to America), also established by the 1964 antipoverty law to enlist volunteers for the antipoverty effort. Although VISTA merged with other volunteer efforts to form the ACTION program in 1971, a large percentage of the agency volunteers remain active on CAA sponsored projects. Their work varies from legal aid to community development to disaster relief. In addition to the regular VISTA volunteers who accounted for 4,400 man-years of service during 1972, some 2,100 students contributed 2,100 more man-years of work in exchange for academic credit in the University Year for Action program.

The OEO legal services program was one of the most significant, and certainly the most controversial programs funded initially as part of CAP. The poor live in the constant shadow of the law. Landlord-tenant problems, wage garnishments for unpaid debts, excessive interest charges and shoddy workmanship from ghetto merchants, and run-ins with the police and juvenile authorities are frequent. Organized legal aid societies have long provided some legal services to the poor, but the legal services program of the Office of Economic Opportunity was the first federal effort to provide better distribution of legal aid.

Most of the cases undertaken by legal services projects were fairly standard matters. Two of every five cases involved family disputes, such as divorce, nonsupport, and custody of children; three in ten, consumer or housing problems; and one in six, noncriminal adult and juvenile proceedings. Of the remaining cases, almost half concerned administrative disputes or decisions by government bureaucracies that affect the poor. Although few in number, these cases attracted the greatest public attention and controversy. In this category legal services may have made the more permanent mark. Among the most far-reaching cases eventually decided by the Supreme Court were those that opened the public assistance rolls to more needy persons.

In its brief, but stormy, history, the legal services program made friends among the poor and disenfranchised but made many enemies in the established power bases. In 1974, after weathering several years of harsh criticism and attempts to weaken the force of the program, an independent Legal Services Corporation was established to take over the legal services program run for the poor by the Office of Economic Opportunity. The new structure provided more direction from the state and national level. Although the vast majority of the cases that legal services handles now are the same kind as before, there are restrictions on the kinds of actions that can be brought against local and state governments and the federal government. Corporation guidelines specifically ban legal services from suing on behalf of its clients for school desegregation or seeking nontherapeutic abortions. There are also bans on political activity, partisan or otherwise, and restrictions on the political activities of legal services attorneys.

Besides supporting the stop-gap approach incorporated in many of the CAP projects, the Great Society policy makers experimented with radical approaches for solving some of the fundamental, chronic problems contributing to poverty. Community Development Corporations (CDCs) were the first sustained effort at building a solid economic base in poor communities. On the federal level these corporations received funding and commitments for support from the Office of Economic Opportunity, the Small Business Administration, and the Department of Housing and Urban Development. At the local level the corporations received enthusiastic moral support from many politicians and community activists and to a lesser extent further financial support.

The CDCs were established to support a variety of community-based enterprises that included manufacturing firms, service ventures, retail establishments, and construction firms. By 1972 the CDCs (as well as many traditional enterprises) were showing a bad record. In the early 1970s the Nixon administration shifted from the CDCs to the Minority Enterprise Small Business Investment Company (MESBIC) as the vehicle for supporting minority enterprise, thus diminishing the community influence in minority enterprises.

The Comprehensive Employment and Training Act of 1973 and the Housing and Community Development Act of 1974 changed the direction of virtually all the Great Society's "community action" strategies. Both acts changed the delivery of federal employment and training funds and community development funds from categorical grants to block grants. The effect of the new thrust has been to place greater reliance on the discretion of local elected officials in deciding how federal funds should be spent. Unfortunately, the change in policy has also put the poor back in a position of being largely dependent upon the good will of local officials.

THE OVERLAP OF CASH AND IN-KIND AID

The overlap of cash and in-kind assistance is inevitable, and, in many cases, desirable. The most obvious—and intended—result is an increase in the economic well-being of recipients. Virtually all public assistance recipients receive medical benefits, 64 percent get food stamps, and 26 percent live in subsidized housing. Some families on public assistance receive none of this in-kind assistance, while others may benefit from several programs. Three-quarters of Old Age and Survivors Insurance recipients are helped by Medicare. Even these limited data show considerable overlap, and complete information would presumably show much more.

Some proponents of in-kind assistance hope that the needy would benefit from as many programs as they qualify for. But there are very serious problems not only in coordinating eligibility for these benefits but in adjusting the level of these benefits as outside earnings change. The present arrangement of administering most of these programs separately exacerbates this problem.

The disincentives have a devastating effect on AFDC families, who are the ones most likely to be able to supplement their assistance with earnings and are also most likely to benefit from one or more in-kind programs. As an AFDC family's earnings rise, it is confronted first of all with a decrease in its assistance payment (losing 67 cents in aid for each dollar earned after the first $30 and work expenses), a social security tax of 5.85 percent on all covered earnings, and federal income tax of at least 16 percent above $6,400 for a family of four. In net cash income alone, an AFDC family receives limited rewards for working.

If the family also receives food stamps, the incentives to work are further diminished. In addition, a most perverse problem arises from Medicaid. This program covers *all* of a beneficiary's medical expenses or none. When a family is no longer eligible, all benefits cease. A family of four that receives the average benefit of $1,227 each year may lose all of this assistance by earning an extra $100. Families who also receive school lunches and public housing are confronted with an even more difficult choice.

The cumulative decrease in benefits as income rises—the cumulative tax rate—is illustrated in table 5. Maintaining meaningful work incentives for a family receiving several forms of aid is one of the thorniest problems in welfare reform.

Given the multiplicity of income support and in-kind programs and the diversity of eligibility rules and certification procedures, there is room for persons to exploit the system and, no doubt, some have. A tendency exists, however, to exaggerate the inequities resulting from duplication. For example, a General Account-

Table 5. Benefits potentially available to a female-headed family of four, 1975

Earnings[a]	AFDC[b]	Taxes		Net Cash	Food Stamp Bonus	Net Cash Plus Food Stamps	Medic-aid[c]
		Soc. Sec.	Income				
—	$2,400	—	—	$2,400	$1,992	$4,392	$1,227
$1,000	2,213	$ 59	—	3,154	1,992	5,146	1,227
2,000	1,547	117	—	3,430	1,752	5,182	1,227
3,000	880	176	—	3,704	1,452	5,156	1,227
4,000	213	234	—	3,979	1,152	5,131	1,227
5,000	—	293	—	4,707	852	5,559	—
6,000	—	351	—	5,649	552	6,201	—
7,000	—	410	$157	6,433	252	6,685	—

[a] According to the U.S. Bureau of Labor Statistics, fringe benefits can add substantially to cash earnings, from $250 at $3,000 earnings to $1,000 at $6,000 earnings.

[b] Assumes the state pays $200 per month and uses the standard "$30 and ⅓" formula, and that the family has work expenses of only $30 per month.

[c] Most states cut off eligibility at an earnings level substantially less than $4,500.

ing Office study found that participation in multiple programs was largely a function of family size—large families face multiple needs and tend, therefore, to participate in more programs. It is doubtful whether a single cash assistance program could provide for all these needs.

ADDITIONAL READINGS

Kamerman, Sheila B. and Kahn, Alfred J. *Social Services in the United States: Policies and Programs.* Philadelphia: Temple University Press, 1976.

Levitan, Sar A. *The Great Society's Poor Law.* Baltimore: The Johns Hopkins University Press, 1969.

Taggart, Robert. *Low Income Housing: A Critique of Federal Aid.* Baltimore: The Johns Hopkins University Press, 1970.

"The Nation's Health: Some Issues," *The Annals*, January 1972.

4

Programs for the Next Generation

Train up a child in the way he should go; and when he is old,
he will not depart from it.

—Proverbs 22:6

Although filling empty bellies in the present is the most pressing
demand on government funds for the poor, it is also important to
take steps to reduce the number of hungry people in the future.
Funds for prevention of poverty may not show definite, positive
results for many years, but they are no less important.

The obvious focus of these efforts are the children of the poor.
Assisting families to limit their family size to their wishes, first of
all, will reduce the number of children who are unwanted and who
cannot be cared for properly. Keeping the mother and child
healthy is necessary for normal physical development regardless of
status. But to prevent future generations from being poor, it is
essential that children from poor families acquire a proper education which would prepare them to function effectively in the job
market.

The provision of these services, like others, is geared to efficiency. Cash assistance to cover birth control information or devices, for instance, would probably not increase their use by the
poor. Birth control devices must be widely distributed, easily available, and highly publicized, and *used* if they are to be effective.

Other services, such as education, are more efficiently provided by the government because of economies of scale, and direct provision is therefore necessary.

BIRTH CONTROL

The close relationship between large families, unwanted births, and poverty is well documented. In 1974, fewer than 10 percent of families with one or two children were in poverty compared with about 16 percent of families with three or four children and 32 percent of families with five or more children. Data support the adage that "the rich get richer and the poor get children." But medical technology is now available to couples to control family size and therefore to alleviate one of the conditions that has often caused poverty.

The misery of many families could have been prevented if practical means for birth control had been provided. Contrary to the widely held misconception that the poor have more children because they want them, a survey of women married between 1966 and 1970 indicated that economic status and race had little bearing on desired family size. All wanted approximately the same number of children, but the poor got more (figure 12).

The 1972 Report of the Presidential Commission on Population Growth and the American Future stated that at least 15 percent of all births between 1966 and 1970 were unwanted and 44 percent were unplanned. The incidence of unwanted births was greater for the lower income and poorly educated population. Twenty percent of births to women with some high school education and 31 percent of births to women with less education were unwanted. Unwanted births over the four-year period numbered about 2.7 million. The evidence is clear that limited access to birth control devices and family planning services has prevented women unable to afford medical care from exercising the same degree of choice as more affluent women.

The reduction of birth rates among the poor would have many positive effects. Fewer children would be born into poor households, and fewer households would be driven into poverty because

87

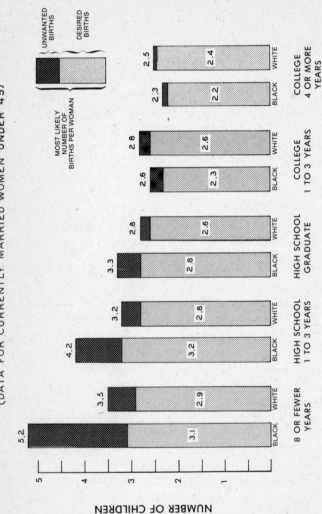

FIGURE 12

FERTILITY AND UNWANTED BIRTHS

(DATA FOR CURRENTLY MARRIED WOMEN UNDER 45)

EDUCATION ATTAINMENT OF MOTHERS

NUMBER OF CHILDREN

of unwanted children. This would help keep people out of poverty, and arrest the acceleration of relief costs.

Lower welfare costs are only a part of the total savings that accrue from birth control programs, just as AFDC payments are only one of the many costs of poverty. Nor are dollar savings the major reason for providing assistance to prevent the birth of unwanted children. The primary goal is the reduction of human misery. Birth control services can, for example, substantially improve health among the poor. By making physical examinations available to low-income women, the presence of cervical cancer and other diseases can be detected and treated. Having too many children too close together is a major contributor to infant mortality, mental retardation, physical defects, and premature births. Frequent pregnancy is recognized as a health hazard to the mother as well, draining her energy, and contributing to high maternal death rates. The Department of Health, Education, and Welfare has confirmed that fertility control is the most effective means of reducing infant death rates and improving maternal and infant health. An additional benefit of fertility control is that children in smaller families tend to receive better care and are less likely candidates for a life of poverty than are children in larger families.

Considering the potential benefits, the costs of a comprehensive birth control program are minimal. It is estimated that more than 6 million poor and near-poor women were in need of organized family planning services in 1975. The cost of providing a patient with a medical examination and birth control devices is about $66 a year. A comprehensive program to furnish services would cost no more than $400 million annually. However, only three-fifths of that was available in 1976 and not all of this amount was used to assist the poor.

American society has undergone dramatic shifts in opinion regarding both birth control and government activity in promoting family planning programs. Attitudes toward termination of unwanted pregnancies through abortion have also softened. A Gallup poll conducted in 1964 indicated that 80 percent of Protestants, 60 percent of Catholics, and 84 percent of persons with other religious preferences favored distribution of birth control information, compared with 86 percent of Protestants, 83 percent of Catholics, and over 95 percent of all others in the 1971 poll. The surveys suggest a tremendous shift in attitudes especially among the young and Catholic populations.

The changing attitudes have had their impact on presidents, Congress, and the courts. While in office, President Eisenhower considered birth control a private matter unfit for public discussion, much less for public support. However, by 1963 he reversed his position and publicly recognized the government's responsibility for population growth and the plight of the poor. President Johnson staunchly supported birth control, in the belief that poor as well as rich families should "have access to information and services that will allow freedom to choose the number and spacing of their children." President Nixon strongly endorsed government family planning activities in his 1969 message on population, stating that "no American woman should be denied access to family planning assistance because of her economic condition." He established the goal of providing family planning services to all indigent women who need and desire them.

The development of this type of legislation reflects the expanded consensus that fertility control is not only a valuable contribution to family life but also an effective measure in preventing poverty. The embryo of federal family planning policies began with Title V of the 1935 Social Security Act. It established formula grants to states for maternal and child health, of which family planning was a component. Congress demonstrated its increased support of the concept in 1967 by earmarking up to 6 percent of Title V funds for family planning and by requiring that birth control services be offered to AFDC mothers under Medicaid.

In response to President Nixon's call for expansion and better integration of family planning services, Congress passed the Family Planning Services and Population Research Act in 1970 to furnish services, conduct research, and develop manpower needed for delivery of services. Expenditures in fiscal 1976 amounted to $101 million. Under Medicaid, the federal contribution makes up 90 percent of outlays. Medicaid agencies were authorized to provide family planning services on a contract basis, and the legislation encouraged delivery of such services to minors. Although Congress placed a ceiling on expenditures for social services in 1972, it exempted family planning services and directed states to offer prompt birth control services to AFDC recipients who desired them, including minors.

Total funding for family planning services rose dramatically between 1968 and 1976 from $16 million to $228 million (excluding payments for services provided by private physicians). Obligations for population and contraception research increased from $8.4 to $51 million in the same time span.

The number of women served by organized programs rose to 3.8 million in 1975, a four-fold rise in seven years. Three of every four clients had incomes of 150 percent of the poverty level or less. An additional 1.3 million low income women received family planning services from private physicians. Despite the rapid expansion of federal family planning services, an estimated 30 percent of eligible low income women of child-bearing age received no subsidized family planning services in 1976. Public assistance recipients made up one in six women served by ongoing programs and accounted for less than one-fourth of eligible women assisted by public welfare.

CHILD CARE

Institutions outside the home are playing an increasingly important role in socializing and educating children and adolescents. However, the home environment still has a fundamental influence on the young, and poverty can seriously and permanently impair their ability to realize educational opportunities. Impoverished children often experience great difficulties during their school years, not only because of health deficiencies and inadequate diet but also because they lack verbal and sensory stimulation in their family environment. Older youths face difficulties in high school and may drop out of school because their motivation and resources are limited. Children from poor families must have special attention from the very start if they are to succeed in school.

Most local institutions are unable or unwilling to offer this assistance. In poor neighborhoods, where schools were typically deficient in resources, facilities, and personnel, the federal government has developed a variety of supportive services to help children from impoverished homes mature into independent adulthood. Such services range from assistance for day care of preschool children to financial support for indigent youths in college (table 6).

Table 6. Estimated federal investment in education for the poor, fiscal 1976

	Outlays (millions)	Percent* to poor
Total	$6,762	37
Elementary and secondary		
Early childhood	456	86
Elementary and secondary education (Title I)	1,900	51
Emergency school aid	258	25
Other	855	21
Higher education		
Supplemental educational opportunity and basic opportunity grants	1,042	37
Work-Study	300	33
TRIO programs	70	81
Student loans	743	20
Educational personnel training and teacher corps	62	57
Other		
Vocational education	552	13
Adult education	64	63
Indian education	285	44
Handicapped	175	20

* Percentage estimates based on 1974 figures.
Source: Derived from Department of Health, Education, and Welfare and Budget of the United States Government.

In 1976 federal sources contributed approximately $2.5 billion to support educational programs focusing on the needs of children and youths from impoverished homes.

Child and Maternal Care

Children's aid programs were the first social welfare services provided by the federal government, dating back to the Taft administration. While child and maternal services are not aimed exclusively at children of poor families, most beneficiaries are from low-income families. A government brochure describing the child welfare services, for example, announces that the program is designed "for troubled children and children in trouble." Problems of child neglect, abuse, and emotional disturbance are not found exclusively in indigent homes, but it is hardly surprising that poor children have more than their share of such problems. Consequently, children from impoverished homes are likely candidates for assistance offered by child welfare programs. In addition, many other poor children who are not public assistance recipients may be beneficiaries of child welfare services administered by state and local welfare agencies and supported by federal grants.

The 1967 amendments to the Social Security Act consolidated health services for mothers, infants, preschool and school children, and crippled children. In addition to maternity and infant care, grants are given to the states for preventive health and care of preschool and school children and for research in these areas. The Office of Child Development, created in 1969, was assigned the responsibility for HEW programs operated on behalf of children. Also placed under its auspices was Head Start, which was transferred from the Office of Economic Opportunity. In addition, the new office was to assume the role of child advocate in the government and promote child development through day care and other child service programs.

"Day care" can mean anything from babysitting to intensive, high quality preschool training and education. At worst, it merely shuffles the child from one destitute household to another, with the loss of personal attention that would come from his own family. At best, day care is provided in well-equipped facilities with experienced staff, offering opportunities for learning, socializing, recreation, and personal care which are unavailable in the home. The cost of comprehensive care runs high, averaging over $200 a month per child.

Federal funding of day care facilities has existed under the Social Security Act since 1962. A significant addition in 1967 was the Work Incentive (WIN) program, which seeks to place "appropriate" adult welfare recipients, including mothers, in training programs and jobs to help them gain economic independence. The legislation requires states to provide child care arrangements for women enrolled in the program. Formal facilities involving large numbers of children and in-home arrangements must meet standards developed by the state. The federal government provides 90 percent of the financing. Day care or "child development" can also be provided as a social service under Aid to Families with Dependent Children. States may set up facilities in poor neighborhoods and provide day care to any child supported by AFDC. These programs may also address themselves to the child's health and general development.

Head Start

A major development in public education during recent years has been the recognition that children from poor homes need preschool programs to compensate for their background deficiencies and to bring them closer to the achievement and adjustment levels of their more affluent peers. The Head Start program was initiated under the 1964 Economic Opportunity Act to meet this need and has become the largest public child-care and development program. Focusing on four- and five-year-old children, the program served 288,000 children in full year programs and 46,000 children in summer programs in 1976 at a total cost of $441 million.

Because Head Start pupils have serious deficiencies, which require individual attention, the program has a lower than usual student-teacher ratio. Like other antipoverty efforts, the program has emphasized the employment of subprofessionals and volunteers to relieve the teacher's work load and provide additional attention to the child. Many of these workers are mothers of children participating in the program. Parental involvement is a major goal of the Head Start effort. A child's needs cannot be met without parental cooperation and, hopefully, beneficial changes in the home environment may be a spin-off effect of the program. Bringing parents into the day-to-day operation of the centers has proved an effective way to advise parents about childrearing practices and to increase their interest in their children's education.

It has been argued that the current educational system acts as a sorting device rather than an equalizing system. Education services are delivered more effectively to children of well-educated and affluent parents than to those of poor parents. Whether Head Start is successful depends ultimately on whether it can induce changes in the American public school system and lessen deleterious influences in home life. More than a shift of goals is necessary, for substantial funds are necessary for the program's continuation. It has been estimated that the cost of compensatory education runs twice as much as the education of children from affluent homes. Indeed, the financial commitment necessary to realize Head Start's goal of quality education for the poor may conceivably lie beyond realistic expectations for the immediate years ahead. Additional research initiatives and parent-child centers explore alternative settings for delivering Head Start services under funding grants totaling $15 million in 1976.

Despite its initial rapid growth, Head Start was able to serve only about 20 percent of eligible children in 1976, and the majority of children attending the program do so only for part of the day. If all eligible children were served in full year programs the price tag would amount to about $3 billion, and additional resources would be needed for personnel development and added facilities.

In an endeavor to provide continuity of effort, Congress approved a Follow Through program in 1967 to extend Head Start services into the early years of primary school. However, the government neglected to provide appropriations for the program, thus limiting it largely to pilot projects. Annual expenditures of up to $60 million supported education or research programs testing the effectiveness of differing educational strategies. The program is to be phased out by 1978.

The magnitude of the task confronting the American educational system has long been recognized, and the competition for scarce educational resources is not a new phenomenon. Head Start has dramatized the educational needs of the poor and sold to the nation a program package whose components provide guidelines for dealing with the poor child's needs. It has attempted to stimulate cognitive development and help disadvantaged children "catch up" with their peers by the time they reach school age. Further, it has challenged local school boards which lacked the understanding, concern, or commitment for the education of the poor. Its impact must ultimately be judged by the changes it induces in the American educational system.

EDUCATION

Elementary and Secondary

The Elementary and Secondary Education Act (ESEA) of 1965 is the primary vehicle for federal support of education for the disadvantaged. Title I of the act provides support of state and local programs for handicapped, delinquent, neglected, and foster children, and for children of migrant workers and Indians and those whose native tongue is not English. It provided $1.6 billion of educational aid in 1976 to school districts enrolling large numbers of poor children. An additional $275 million was expended in grants to states to help children in state-operated institutions.

Unlike Head Start, which distributes funds on a project-by-project basis with detailed guidelines for localities to follow, Title I funds are distributed in a block grant to state educational authorities, who then disburse them to local school boards. In 1976 funds were allocated to 13,000 school systems and were focused on the educational needs of 4.5 million children. The average expenditure of $360 per child was utilized for additional education materials, teacher's aides, speech and reading specialists, and other services. ESEA has directed funds into poor districts and opened possibilities for compensatory education, although some of the funds have been used to help nonpoor children or have been misdirected for other purposes.

Post Secondary

Although its value in the marketplace may be diminishing, the sheepskin is still one of the surest avenues out of poverty. However, only 24 percent of youths from families whose income is below $5,000 go to college compared with one-third of youths from families whose income is between $5,000 and $10,000 and over half the offspring of families whose annual income is over $15,000 (figure 13). Youths from poor families face an educational obstacle course featuring insufficient money, lack of motivation, and low quality education in areas where the poor are concentrated. Upward Bound, Talent Search, and Special Services—the TRIO programs administered by the Office of Education—are designed to help disadvantaged students over some of the hurdles to higher educational achievement.

The Upward Bound program seeks to motivate students early in their high school careers and to help set their sights on college. Institutions of higher education receive grants to offer summer training and remedial education, including residence on a college campus, as well as tutoring throughout the school year. Most students enter after the tenth or eleventh grade and attend two or three summer sessions before entering college. Special projects for veterans have been in effect since 1972, and they accounted in 1974 for one-fourth of those served.

Current appropriations are adequate to serve only 12 to 15 percent of the estimated 360,000 students eligible for Upward Bound. At the average cost of $968 per student, only 44,000 were served in 1974. In 1975 the number served increased to 53,000 but at a lower average expenditure per student.

Six of every ten Upward Bound high school graduates have entered college. Sixty percent of those who entered college in 1970 were still enrolled two years later, indicating that Upward Bounders are as likely to remain in college as other students. The effectiveness of Upward Bound also suggests that the program has selected students with maximum potential. If funds were available to help more youths from poor homes, the proportion entering college would undoubtedly drop. But the success of the Upward Bound program so far indicates that motivational problems and educational obstacles to higher education can be overcome.

Talent Search is a related program designed to identify poor youths with exceptional potential for higher education and to make them aware of financial assistance sources. Although several mil-

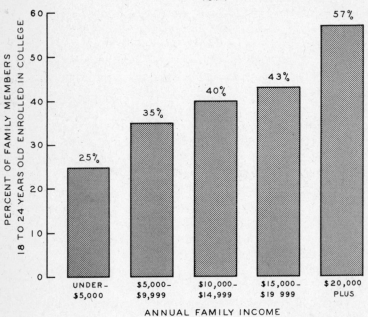

FIGURE 13
COLLEGE ENROLLMENT AND FAMILY INCOME
1974

PERCENT OF FAMILY MEMBERS
18 TO 24 YEARS OLD ENROLLED IN COLLEGE

60 — 57%

50 —

43%

40% 40 —

35%

30 —

25% 20 —

10 —

0 —

| UNDER– | $5,000– | $10,000– | $15,000– | $20,000 |
| $5,000 | $9,999 | $14,999 | $19 999 | PLUS |

ANNUAL FAMILY INCOME

Source: U.S. Bureau of the Census

lion students were eligible for referral, 146,000 were singled out in 1975 by Talent Search, at a cost of about $47 per student. Talent Search, as the title suggests, seeks out gifted but financially strapped students and offers them information to clear the path to higher education. Since 1972 special emphasis has been placed on identifying veterans.

Special Services for Disadvantaged Students are designed to help poor youths remain in college once they get there. In 1975 approximately 100,000 students received remedial and tutorial services at an average cost of $230 per student.

While there are many private scholarships based on need, they are usually limited to the most gifted students. The student of average potential who lives in poverty has little hope of receiving support. The federal government funds two programs that are of interest to such students. Most colleges participate in the work-study program that allows students to work up to 15 hours a week during the regular school year and up to 40 hours a week in summer work programs. The rates of pay are determined by the colleges. In 1976 the government allocated $570 million to aid 973,000 students in this way. An average of $520 was added to the student's annual income in exchange for work on campus or for another nonprofit institution. The initial federal contribution of 80 percent was cut by 1976 to 70 percent, and Ford administration spokesmen favored further reduction of the federal share to 50 percent of total outlays. Eligibility requirements have been relaxed since the program's initiation as part of antipoverty efforts in 1964, and only one of every three participants is from a poor home.

The Higher Education Act of 1965 also provided poor students with annual grants ranging from $200 to $1,000 which the institutions they attend must match. The $240 million distributed in 1976 assisted 447,000 students who received an average grant of $670. Most grants are awarded to students from poor or near-poor families. Nearly three of every five beneficiaries were members of families with an annual income of less than $6,000.

The 1972 amendments to the Higher Education Act authorized basic opportunity grants of $1,400 a year for every poor student in post secondary education. The grant would be reduced by the amount the family could afford to contribute to the student's education. These grants have become the largest single mechanism for aiding low income students funneling $1 billion to 1,268,000 students in 1976 with average grants of $789. Funds were provided to an estimated three-fourths of eligible recipients. Three in ten recipients lived in families with incomes of less than $3,000 and almost six in ten come from families in the less than $6,000 annual income. While the basic opportunity grants are directed toward students from impoverished homes, they open funding to middle income students, especially if parents do not claim income tax deductions for their children.

In addition, the amendments also instituted supplemental educational opportunity grants to replace the educational opportunity grants program, increasing the annual grant limit to $1,500 per year. The program acted in tandem with the basic opportunity grants to meet the costs of school attendance for the very poor, especially those attending high-cost institutions. However supplemental opportunity grants are scheduled for termination by 1977 because they duplicated basic opportunity grants. Increased funding will be made available under the latter program to cover those who would have benefited under the supplemental opportunity grants. A projected total of 1.5 million students will receive basic opportunity grants for the 1977–78 school year.

Incentive grants to state institutions provide matching funds to states on a 50-50 basis to support needy students as defined by state standards. In 1976 the federal contribution reached $44 million and aided an estimated 176,000 students. However, fewer than one in three was poor.

The federal grants initiated by the Great Society antipoverty legislation in 1964 have expanded during the succeeding dozen years and have gone a long way toward enabling aspiring youths from impoverished homes to complete a college education. Combined with state supported colleges and universities, the GI bill, and private scholarships, financial need is no longer a decisive deterrent to the acquisition of a college education in the United States.

ADDITIONAL READINGS

Levitan, Sar A. and Alderman, Karen Cleary. *Child Care and ABCs Too.* Baltimore: The Johns Hopkins University Press, 1975.

Mosteller, Frederick and Moynihan, Daniel P. (eds.). *On Equality of Educational Opportunity.* New York: Vintage Books, 1972.

Population and the American Future. The Report of the Commission on Population Growth and the American Future. Washington: Government Printing Office, 1972.

Silberman, Charles E. *Crisis in the Classroom.* New York: Random House, 1970.

Sowell, Thomas. *Black Education: Myth and Tragedies.* New York: David McKay & Co., 1972.

Wirtz, Willard. *The Boundless Resource.* Washington: New Republic, 1975.

5

Programs for the Employable Poor

Anticipate charity by preventing poverty; assist the reduced
fellowman . . . so that he may earn an honest livelihood, and not be
forced to the dreadful alternative of holding out his hand for charity.
This is the highest step and the summit of charity's golden ladder.
                                        —Moses ben Maimon

Direct cash payments and the provision of goods and services
lessen the burden of poverty but do not attack the causes of dependency. Programs that provide opportunities for self-support
and permanent exits from poverty are also needed. As an old
proverb moralizes, "Give a man a fish and you feed him for a day.
Teach him to catch a fish and you feed him for life."

Those in need of self-help programs are found in a variety of
situations. Some of the unemployed lack the skills to compete
effectively in the labor market and others are qualified workers
unable to locate a demand for their skill. There are also some, not
counted among the unemployed, who are too discouraged by their
failure to find work to continue to look. In addition, there are
employed persons counted among the "working poor." They are
part-time workers who need full-time work to keep them out of
poverty and persons employed at such low wages that even full-
time work does not raise them above the poverty standard. These
underemployed and low earners, when added to the unemployed

and discouraged, constitute the "subemployed." The subemployment rate may be more than double the reported unemployment rate, and gives a more realistic indication of the universe of need for manpower services.

The range of self-help programs for the employable poor is wide. Some programs focus on the supply side of the labor market, preparing the poor for gainful employment. These include the majority of the employment and training programs launched in the 1960s. Other programs are directed to the demand side, opening doors for the poor in the private labor market and providing public employment for those who are not absorbed in the private sector. A third group of programs seeks to improve the functioning of the labor market for the poor, matching up supply and demand more effectively and setting standards and minimums for low-income employment. Finally, several programs deal with all three of these aspects of the labor market, but concentrate on a specific geographical area or population group.

EMPLOYMENT AND TRAINING

Employment and training programs provide a wide variety of labor market services and carry a substantial price tag—amounting in 1976 to $9 billion (table 7). They include efforts directed to specific categories of clients as well as comprehensive programs with broad eligibility criteria. In varying combinations, the following labor market services are offered:

1. outreach to identify the untrained and undermotivated as well as intake and assessment to evaluate their needs and abilities;

2. adult basic education to remedy the absence or obsolescence of earlier schooling;

3. prevocational orientation to expose those of limited experience to alternative occupational choices;

4. training persons lacking a rudimentary education for entry level skills;

5. residential facilities for those who live in sparsely populated areas or who have a home environment that would adversely affect attempts to overcome their disadvantages;

Table 7. Federal outlays for employment and training programs, 1964, 1970, and 1976 (millions)

Activity	1964	1970	1976 (est.)
Total	$450	$2,546	$9,053
Institutional training	105	614	959
On-the-job training	5	280	532
Vocational rehabilitation	96	494	892
In-school work support	——	263	547
Postschool work support	——	220	956
Public service employment	——	——	3,418
Labor market services (job placement and antidiscrimination)	184	391	769
Child care and other	37	141	784
Administration, research, and miscellaneous	23	143	196

Source: U.S. Office of Management and Budget

6. work experience for those unaccustomed to the discipline of the work place;

7. creation of public service jobs to upgrade the skills of the disadvantaged until they can compete for permanent public careers;

8. countercyclical creation of public employment opportunities to absorb jobless workers in a high unemployment economy;

9. subsidized private employment for the disadvantaged;

10. job placement and labor market information services;

11. job coaching to work out supervisor-worker relationships once a job is found;

12. job development efforts to solicit job opportunities suited to the abilities of the disadvantaged job seeker;

13. training allowances to provide support and incentives for those undergoing training; and

14. supportive services—such as medical aid and day care centers for mothers with small children—for those who need assistance to facilitate entry or resumption of work.

Despite the large price tag and the wide variety of available labor market services, employment and training programs are adequate only to help a small proportion of the people who need such services (table 8). Few projects, if any, offer all the listed services,

Table 8. Enrollment in federal employment and training programs, fiscal 1975 (thousands)

Total	*1,986*
Vocational rehabilitation	802
Skill training	*532*
Institutional	374
On-the-job	158
Job creation	*652*
Work experience	496
Public service	156

Source: U.S. Office of Management and Budget

and participants rarely receive the precise package they need. Complementary programs are insufficiently coordinated, and the individual may be ineligible or unaware of needed programs because of their diversity.

Nevertheless, those who are served can benefit greatly. The programs can improve earning capacity and help people to rise out of dependency. This is in fact the goal of these self-help programs, as stated in the preamble to the Economic Opportunity Act of 1964: "It is . . . the policy of the United States to eliminate the paradox of poverty in the midst of plenty in this Nation by opening to everyone the opportunity to live in decency and dignity."

Disadvantaged workers have serious deficiencies which make them unattractive to employers. Most are poorly educated and unskilled, and some are unaccustomed to the world of work. Basic education, vocational training, counseling, and work experience help make the poor more attractive to potential employers. According to the service provided, current manpower programs can be divided into two major groups: those that emphasize training (including remediation) and those that stress work experience and job creation. Because a comparison of services provided under either category reveals overlap, the breakdown is based more on actual performance than on goals.

Vocational Education and Rehabilitation

Vocational education is the oldest federal investment in job-related training, dating back to 1917. Federal expenditures in fiscal year 1976 totaled about $550 million, and state and local governments contributed over four times as much. Four-fifths of the federal share was for matching grants to states for basic vocational education programs; the rest supported grants to states for consumer and homemaking education, work-study, cooperative education, vocational research, and other specific activities. Most of the federal money is distributed in grants to state governments, which then parcel it out to local school districts. State and local officials traditionally had wide latitude in spending these funds. In an attempt to gain some control, Congress required in the 1968 Vocational Education Amendments that 15 percent of the state grant be spent for disadvantaged and another 10 percent for handicapped students. However, most school systems have tended to define "disadvantaged" broadly and have included many students who do not come from poor families. Inadequate records are kept by the states about student or program characteristics. Furthermore, some states have not been careful to restrict these monies to the designated students. Thus, help for the poor has probably not yet matched congressional intent.

In addition to these earmarked funds are the regular classes, which enroll the bulk of the students. Because students from poor families are considerably more likely to enroll in a vocational curriculum and are less likely to continue their education beyond high school, it is important that vocational courses that would qualify them for jobs be available to them. Although enrollments have been shifting toward more saleable skills, many students attend schools that offer few choices and quite a few are enrolled in courses that may offer little job-related training. Of the total 13.6 million enrollment in 1974, one student in four was enrolled in home economics and almost one in ten in agriculture. Although these curricula are more job-related than in the past, these two categories represent a large number of students whose employment potential is not being increased. On the other hand, federal matching is now available for office, technical, and health occupational and training programs with a 1974 enrollment in excess of 3.7 million. It is important that vocational education keep pace with the rapidly changing job market in order to provide useful skills.

Many vocational education enrollees are adults, but most are not poor. The educational needs of poor adults are more directly addressed by the $70 million Adult Basic Education program administered by HEW's Office of Education. Because almost half of the heads of poor families have completed eight years of schooling or less, it is obvious that the poor form a large proportion of the 700,000 enrollees in adult basic education courses. A number of the enrollees go on to job training programs, and many others benefit directly from their educational improvements by higher income.

Job training as well as medical, educational, and other needed services are offered to the physically and mentally handicapped under the federally-supported vocational rehabilitation programs. During fiscal 1975, 1.3 million persons received such services, and more than 306,000 were rehabilitated. In 1965 impoverishment was included as a category of disabling mental handicaps. It was reasoned that the case-by-case approach of vocational rehabilitation, which provides a variety of services according to individual needs, would prove an effective means of preparing disadvantaged people for satisfactory employment. While few persons are selected on the basis of poverty alone, many of the disabled are poor. The mean household income of the 7.7 million adults in 1972 unable to work regularly or at all because of persistent chronic ailments was half that of the nondisabled.

The vocational rehabilitation program has thus played a significant role in preventing poverty. Seven of every ten participants in the program were successfully rehabilitated, i.e., were placed in jobs or improved their homemaking capability. Four of five rehabilitants had no earnings at entry, while the average weekly earnings for the group was only $14. At closure, 85 percent received wages, and the average weekly earnings for the group had increased more than fivefold to $76. The proportion of rehabilitants receiving public assistance fell by half from 17 to 8 percent. The mean cost per client was $2,800 per rehabilitant.

One can only speculate whether the successes of the vocational rehabilitation program would be achieved if it were extended to more of the severely disabled with low income or to poor persons generally, but the existing program is effectively enhancing the employability of a large number of physically and mentally handicapped poor people, and it is preventing others from becoming economically dependent.

Skill Training

Skill training was the focus of most manpower programs in the 1960s. A wide variety of programs was developed as new problems were recognized, and by the early 1970s there was a clear need to consolidate and coordinate the diverse efforts. The Comprehensive Employment and Training Act (CETA) of 1973 was enacted to decategorize and decentralize most of these programs—to remove federal strictures on program structure and to vest greater planning and implementing authority in state and local governments. But despite the advent of the newly designed federal-state-local partnership, CETA's first few years brought few major changes in program structure.

The first major training program initiated in the 1960s—the Manpower Development and Training Act of 1962—provided institutional training for the unemployed and underemployed. Though the original emphasis was upon retraining technologically displaced workers with long labor force attachment, MDTA was amended to give increased recognition to employment problems of the disadvantaged. The institutional programs were expanded to include basic education; training allowances were increased in both amount and duration; and skills centers were established in some 80 communities to provide institutional training in a variety of occupations along with supportive services. Follow-up studies show that most enrollees benefited from their training experience. They experienced less unemployment than did control groups, and their earnings increased.

Even under the CETA block grant approach to states and localities, the federal government maintained direct responsibilities for Indians, migrants, and seasonal workers, and the Job Corps program.

The Job Corps, established by the Economic Opportunity Act

of 1964, provides intensive and expensive vocational training and basic education to youths from 16 to 21 years of age, although 14- and 15-year-olds may qualify. Largely a residential program, it rests on the assumption that the most seriously disadvantaged young people must be removed from their debilitating home environments before they can be rehabilitated. Almost all Job Corps enrollees are from poor families, and most suffer serious educational deficiencies which would certainly sentence them to a life of poverty. Many have failed in other training or jobs.

All enrollees receive basic education through teaching techniques especially developed for the disadvantaged. On the average, they benefit more from this training than they did from their public schools, with educational gains approaching public school norms. Vocational training of differing complexity is provided, and the corpsmen receive a wide variety of supportive services, including room, board, health care, recreation, and allowances. The total cost of these services is high—approximately $5,000 per enrollee in fiscal 1976 for an average length of stay of slightly less than six months—but largely unavoidable if residential training is to be provided to hard-core, unemployed, out-of-school youth. The Job Corps operated about 60 centers in 1976, and enrolled about 46,000 youths, the bulk from impoverished homes.

Since the end of World War II, the Veterans Administration has administered financial support for ex-servicemen who wish to continue their education or training. Monthly stipends of $270 for single veterans ($321 for a veteran with one dependent) have been utilized predominantly by college enrollees; apprenticeship and on-the-job training programs have not been as popular. Moreover, the educationally disadvantaged and black veterans have failed to participate in the same proportions as white and high school graduate veterans. To encourage disadvantaged veterans to benefit from the programs, a 1970 amendment to the law provided that time spent on remedial courses or tutoring to correct an educational deficiency could be added to the entitlement, with no reduction in the 36-month limit on benefits. About 291,000 veterans with less than a high school education benefited from the program by mid-1974.

Job Creation

Job creation—known variously as public service employment or work experience—came into its own in the 1970s as an integral part of manpower policy. Throughout the 1960s the increasing panoply of programs focused largely on the supply side of the labor market, by increasing the employability of the unemployed and underemployed. With a few notable exceptions, there was little attention to the demand side, by increasing the number of jobs for those available for work.

The largest job creation effort during the 1960s was the Neighborhood Youth Corps, established under the Economic Opportunity Act, which consisted of three separate but related programs aimed at providing work experience and income support for poor youths: summer and in-school programs to provide jobs and income, with the hope of encouraging youths to remain in school, and an out-of-school program which provided an "aging vat," as well as some training, to high school dropouts.

Although the evidence is mixed, NYC was of value in introducing disadvantaged youths to the responsibilities of a job. Some findings indicated that the participants in the in-school and summer programs did not have lower high school dropout rates. But even if the income did not improve educational performance, it was justified for the assistance provided to the needy.

At the other end of the age spectrum, Operation Mainstream provided public employment for middle-aged and older unemployed workers stranded in rural areas. Most of the work in rural areas was in conservation; urban programs included social service aides. Little training was offered to the older participants, but for the many elderly participants, the earnings were a needed supplement to social security payments, and, perhaps of equal importance, they fostered a sense of productivity rather than dependence.

More promising employment opportunities directed at the general population were offered by the Public Service Careers program, which placed enrollees in paraprofessional jobs with public and private nonprofit agencies dealing in human services—health, education, welfare, and housing. In 1970, the program began to encourage federal, state, and local governments to hire and train or to upgrade the disadvantaged.

Through the 1960s job creation efforts were limited in scope and target groups. In contrast, the Emergency Employment Act of 1971 funded public employment jobs on a much larger scale as a countercyclical tool to combat high unemployment. The $2.5 billion expended under the act over a three-year period created, at its peak in 1972, a total of 170,000 jobs. The law allocated the funds directly to the states and communities to pay the wages of those hired. The public employment program was not intended to be solely an antipoverty program. As a result, only one in five jobs created were filled by disadvantaged individuals. The program was successful in gearing up quickly to hire the unemployed, but its success was modest in effecting its secondary goals of restructuring jobs, initiating civil service reforms, aiding depressed areas, and providing transition to permanent employment. Changes in these areas would have resulted in more long-run improvements in the employment status of the poor.

Enactment of the Comprehensive Employment and Training Act in 1973 made little immediate change in these job-creation efforts. The Neighborhood Youth Corps, Operation Mainstream, and Public Service Careers programs were incorporated into the act's sweeping Title I. However, the federal government continued to provide funds specifically for summer youth programs (nearly $500 million in 1976) and also for Operation Mainstream projects. Title II of CETA was patterned closely after the 1971 job-creation program and was notable as an ongoing major ($400 million a year) public employment effort aimed at the structurally unemployed.

High unemployment in the mid-1970s led to enactment in 1974 of a much larger public service employment program under Title VI of CETA aimed at the recession's victims. Some $2.5 billion was appropriated for 1975. Together, with some Title I funds allocated for job creation, CETA supported about 300,000 jobs in 1975.

However, with vast numbers of unemployed persons with good work histories, state and local employing agencies gave short shrift

111

to persons in poverty and members of minority groups. This problem was exacerbated by the financial straits of many local governments that used much of their funds to rehire laid-off employees who were not counted among the disadvantaged.

Delivery Agencies

Besides the shortage of jobs and lack of skills, the employable poor also suffer because they are unaware both of existing employment opportunities and of training programs. The labor market does not perfectly coordinate jobs with workers, and its inefficiencies are most noticeable in serving poor people.

The largest single delivery system of labor market services is the United States Employment Service (USES). Its 2,400 local offices placed 3.1 million individuals in 1975, including 900,000 poor persons. Disadvantaged applicants have constituted close to one-fifth of the total in each year since 1968 when the statistics were first collected. One reason for the overrepresentation of the disadvantaged recently has been the "work test" of the food stamp, welfare, and unemployment insurance programs which require employable applicants to register for work at the USES. Though federally financed, the USES is administered separately in each state. As a result, services to the poor may vary significantly from state to state and from local office to local office.

The Great Society antipoverty efforts shifted the emphasis and responsibilities of the public employment offices toward aid for the poor. The volume of USES activity declined largely because of this shift in emphasis away from serving employers and towards helping the disadvantaged. In the 1970s the ES attempted to rebuild its employer services by reaching out to nondisadvantaged applicants who could fill more of the available job opportunities and by advertising the benefits of this free "job service" to employers to secure more listings.

As the public employment service was attempting through more efficient management to regain its former position in the labor market, enactment in 1973 of CETA created a new obstacle. The employment service had been the presumptive deliverer of outreach, counseling, placement, and other services prior to 1973.

But state and local officials funded under CETA had the option of using other organizations to provide these services. The employment service accordingly lost some ground, especially in urban areas.

The Work Incentive (WIN) program is the culmination of efforts since the early 1960s to induce welfare recipients to achieve economic independence and to stem the growth of welfare. Experience has shown the difficulty of achieving these goals. Enacted as a 1967 amendment to the Social Security Act, WIN began by promising maximum services to each enrollee. Because enrollees often needed basic education and skill training, as well as child care and other supportive services, success was modest and costs were high. Indeed, many "graduates" did not earn enough to leave the welfare rolls.

In reaction to such limited results, the Talmadge amendments, which took effect beginning in 1973, increased federal matching to make the program more attractive to states, and deemphasized classroom training in favor of immediate employment through on-the-job training, work support, and direct job placement. But even this formulation was not satisfactory, and the proportion of funds spent on skill training dropped steadily, while the proportion spent on job placement rose. By fiscal 1976, total expenditures were $350 million—$235 million for training and job placement and $115 million for child care and other services. But classroom training, which accounted for nearly all the training expenditures in fiscal 1972, comprised only one-eighth of the 1976 total, and registration for work and direct job placement accounted for nearly half of the 1976 total.

WIN was less and less a training program, and more and more a delivery agency. In fiscal 1976 over 500,000 persons were called in for registration and development of employability plans, and an estimated 200,000 persons were placed in jobs, but many of these persons would probably have found jobs on their own. Although the volume of WIN activity has increased substantially, it is not clear that there remains much substance to the program. Because WIN provides little upgrading of enrollees, even those who are placed in jobs leave the program with the same meager skills with which they started. The program provides, therefore, a limited exit from poverty and dependence.

The first steps have been taken in consolidating manpower resources and allowing local authorities greater freedom to determine their needs in spending available federal funds, yet there remains much to do. In many areas the decentralization and decategorization under CETA effected little substantial change. In any case, WIN, the employment service, vocational education, and veterans programs still operate independently of CETA and of each other. The budget stringencies of the 1970s make effective coordination all the more important.

EQUAL OPPORTUNITY IN EMPLOYMENT

Job discrimination has been a major cause of poverty among blacks, Chicanos, and other minority groups. Some among the poor have been denied jobs or advancement solely because of their race, color, or national origin. Title VII of the Civil Rights Act of 1964 bans discriminatory employment practices by employers, labor organizations, registered apprenticeship programs, and employment services hiring or serving 15 or more persons. In 1972 coverage was expanded to public as well as private employers.

The five-member Equal Employment Opportunity Commission (EEOC) was created to implement Title VII. Charged with processing complaints on a case-by-case basis, and constrained initially to settle cases through voluntary compliance, the EEOC's powers were extended in 1972 to seek court orders against respondents found to be in violation of the law. The courts also broadened the definition of discrimination and the employer's liability for such acts. In 1971 the Supreme Court ruled that practices which were fair in form, but discriminatory in operation, were illegal. Specifically, it outlawed preemployment tests that were not job-related on the grounds that they were more likely to exclude blacks and other minorities. The court expanded this reasoning in proscribing the use of arrest records to screen employees. In another important 1971 decision the court established the principle of class action and large reparations as discrimination cases, raising the ante in civil rights litigation.

Though the EEOC has never been granted power to issue cease-and-desist orders, it has steadily expanded its size and enforcement activities. In fiscal 1971 the commission completed 7,320 investigations at a cost of $16 million. By fiscal 1975, 33,000 cases were handled at a cost of $55 million. The EEOC's staff of lawyers was increased more than fivefold in 1973 in order to utilize its newly legislated authority. In a landmark case, the American Telephone and Telegraph Company signed a consent decree in 1973 involving $15 million in restitution and back pay for several classes of female employees and a $23 million promotion package for women and minorities. This agreement was the first shot in a stepped up campaign that resulted in a number of large settlements.

Another approach was to use the substantial market leverage of the government. The Office of Federal Contract Compliance (OFCC), an arm of the U.S. Department of Labor created by executive order in 1965, requires all federal contractors to establish affirmative action goals and timetables. The major action has been in the area of construction. In 1969 the Department of Labor issued the Philadelphia plan requiring construction contractors in that city to increase the proportion of minority craftsmen from 2 percent up to 4 to 9 percent in the first year and 19 to 26 percent by the fourth year. The Supreme Court approved this approach and similar plans were implemented in a number of cities. Rarely did these achieve targeted employment goals but they apparently increased minority hiring at union wage levels.

Despite reluctance to use its full powers, OFCC pressure has had an effect on employment. Between 1966 and 1970 firms with government contracts increased their employment of black males by 3.3 percent more than those not doing business with the federal government. Government contractors with no black employees in 1966 were 10 percent more likely by 1970 to have hired at least one black male. Overall the wage share of black workers in the average firm with government contracts increased by 28 percent between 1966 and 1970, compared with 25 percent in the other firms.

Minimum Wages

The persistence of poverty among the working poor testifies to the failure of existing institutions and the need for their improvement. In April 1971 there were an estimated 5.8 million full-time jobs in the private nonfarm sector paying less than the $2.00 per hour needed to bring a family of four—assuming that the employee worked more than 2,000 hours annually—close to the then poverty threshold.

Though most of these low-paying jobs are filled on a part-time basis by secondary earners, or by youths, there are also a significant number of family heads who work regularly but are unable to rise out of poverty. In 1974, there were almost 1 million poor families whose head (90 percent of whom were males) held a full-time job all year. There were also nearly 300,000 unrelated individuals working full-time, full year, but remaining in poverty (figure 14). Higher hourly wages would, of course, be required to raise them above the poverty line.

The plight of these working poor receives little attention in the training and public employment programs already described. These programs tend to be preoccupied with the unemployed, youth, and those outside the labor force. The goal of most of training programs is full-time employment; that this may be no real solution to poverty is often ignored, as are the needs of those who are already laboring at full-time, low-paying jobs.

The minimum wage is perhaps the most direct and comprehensive measure to increase the earnings of the working poor. The objective of the Fair Labor Standards Act of 1938 was to achieve, as rapidly as practicable, minimum wage levels that would sustain the health, efficiency, and general well-being of all workers. An unduly high or rapidly rising minimum might price many low-productivity jobs out of existence, so that the gains from higher wages had to be balanced against the losses from job elimination.

On the assumption that a low-paying job is better than no job at all, Congress has acted incrementally in applying the law over the years. It has established minimum wages that directly affect only a limited number of employees at the bottom of the economic lad-

FIGURE 14
WORK EXPERIENCE OF THE POOR
1974

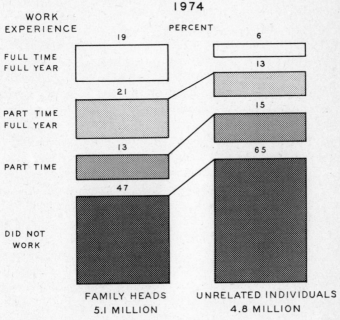

WORK
EXPERIENCE
PERCENT

FULL TIME
FULL YEAR

PART TIME
FULL YEAR

PART TIME

DID NOT
WORK

FAMILY HEADS
5.1 MILLION

UNRELATED INDIVIDUALS
4.8 MILLION

Source: U.S. Bureau of the Census

der. The 1974 amendments expanded minimum wage protection to an additional 7.4 million workers, bringing the total number of covered nonsupervisory workers to 56.8 million. The two major groups covered by the 1974 amendments were federal, state, and local employees and most private household workers. Still not covered are 9.4 million nonsupervisory employees, primarily in retail and wholesale trade, service industries, agriculture, finance, and manufacturing. Though state minimum wage laws provide some protection to excluded workers, these standards range widely and are usually far below the federal minimum wage.

The 1974 amendments increased the minimum hourly wage for employees in already-covered industries to $2.30 in January 1976. Employees in newly-covered industries were to reach the $2.30 level in January 1977, while covered agricultural employees were to reach that level in January 1978.

One can only speculate about the number of workers whose earnings are boosted by minimum wage, but some insights can be gained from reviewing the incremental increases in the minimum wage and extensions in coverage. It was estimated that the 1974 law boosted the wages of 4.2 million workers.

The favorable impact of minimum wage rates is reduced to the extent that employers find it unprofitable to retain or hire workers at the government-imposed wage levels, resulting in unemployment rather than higher earnings. Because many factors are involved, it is difficult to determine the extent of job elimination. The available evidence indicates that the minimum wage legislation has raised the total income of the poor, and that any losses in employment and earnings were more than compensated by the increased earnings of the majority. This is, of course, little comfort to individuals who lost their jobs as a result of such increases. Nor do studies of changes affecting those presently employed tell the whole story. Future demand for labor might be dampened, closing off potential job opportunities for those who might otherwise have been hired. Some economists claim that the youth unemployment problem is largely the result of minimum wages. If minimum wages were reduced or removed altogether, they argue, more jobs would be created at lower wages. The assertion remains unproven but there is some evidence that it holds true for those youths of minority groups. Accordingly, support has developed for a "dual minimum," which would permit a lower minimum, for example, for all youths under 18, full-time students under 20, and 18- to 19-year-olds in the first six months of employment.

It is questionable, however, whether a dual minimum wage would have a significant impact on youth unemployment. A major cause of unemployment among black teenagers and other disadvantaged groups must be sought elsewhere. First, the liberalization and expansion of various income support measures, including Aid to Families with Dependent Children, has offered a minimal measure of income maintenance to young women with children. Some may have preferred to subsist on relief rather than to work at very low wages. Second, many of the potential jobs open to blacks in slum areas disappeared with the exodus of white families. As jobs moved to suburbia, many residents of slum areas became economically stranded, owing to inadequate public transportation or the lack of private "wheels." In other words, some black unemployment reflects suburban housing discrimination. Third, demographic factors and an increased supply of black youths in slum areas must also have contributed to increased unemployment, particularly since, as already suggested, the demand for their labor has declined. Nonetheless, if a significant boost in minimum wages can be purchased at some inflationary cost, the trade-off may be a small price to help reduce the number of working poor. In the final analysis conclusions regarding the impact of minimum wage legislation upon aggregate employment and unemployment depend on value judgments, and whatever the conclusion some relevant facts can be found to support the views.

To minimize the dangers of unemployment and inflationary pressures, many proponents concede that minimum wages should be raised no more rapidly than average wages in American industry. While little is known about productivity trends in low-wage industries affected by minimum wage legislation, it is reasonable to assume that the rise in productivity in these industries is no greater than in the rest of the American economy. If this assertion is correct, a rule of thumb might be that boosts in the minimum wage should be no larger than rises in the cost of living, plus average productivity increases.

In an inflationary economy it may be desirable to raise the minimum rate frequently, at least more often than Congress is likely to enact new legislation. One way to adjust the minimum wage to increasing living costs, and to avoid the discontinuities of infrequent but large jumps, is to "index" the minimum to a cost-of-living measure, much as social security and other benefits are now automatically increased.

Some experts have argued for setting minimum wage rates high enough to eliminate poverty among all full-time workers. Regrettably such pronouncements are more rhetoric than serious policy alternatives. Reasonable people may differ on whether the current minimum wage should be extended to additional millions of workers or whether it should be kept for a while at the present level or raised by a few cents, but there can be little doubt that excessively rapid boosts in the minimum wage would cause serious economic dislocations and loss of jobs. It would be a case of killing the goose that lays the egg, even if it contains little gold. Eliminating jobs is not the way to fight poverty. Rapid increases in minimum wages, in any event, should be accompanied by a work relief program that would provide employment to displaced workers at the statutory minimum wage rate.

Without diminishing the past achievements of the minimum wage, it would be unrealistic to place excessive reliance upon such legislation as a tool to combat poverty. If society is determined to reduce poverty at a more rapid rate than in the past, additional tools will have to be relied upon.

Migrant Workers and Illegal Immigrants

As a group, migrant workers are one of the most exploited segments of the work force. Most are blacks and Mexican-Americans based in southern Texas, California, and Florida. The average migrant worker has only a fourth or fifth grade education. Living conditions are normally characterized by substandard housing, both in base residence and while traveling. Dilapidated housing, low incomes, and a lack of protection from employment-related injury and illness foster poor health conditions. These workers follow the harvest as far north as Minnesota, Washington, and New York each year, often paying farm labor contractors to find them jobs at wages bringing an average annual income of less than $3,000.

Because they are on the move from spring until fall each year, migrant workers are difficult to reach through the standard federal social and welfare programs. Residency requirements and difficulties in certifying their incomes limit their access to such programs as Medicaid, food stamps, welfare, and job training. Given their meager incomes, child labor becomes a necessity in defiance of laws designed to keep the children in school. In 1970, over one-third of the 196,000 migrant workers were between 14 and 17 years old. Therefore, the schooling of children of these families is a primary concern.

Employment prospects for migrant workers are declining steadily as more mechanical devices are introduced in the harvesting process. There has been no significant increase in rural nonfarm employment to absorb displaced workers. Moreover, these working poor are not entitled to the protection of federal labor laws providing for unemployment compensation and collective bargaining or of many states' workers' compensation laws. Therefore, the need to train migrant workers and to provide basic education to their children is pressing if the poverty of these families is not to be visited on future generations.

Even the serious problems of migrant laborers are probably not as severe as those of illegal immigrants. Foreign nationals who enter the United States without proper documents typically suffer the worst working conditions and the lowest wages of any segment of the labor force. Yet, because they are outside the law, they have no redress for their grievances, little access to public aid or institutional support, and neither the education nor the incentive to openly protest the exploitation, extortion, and fraud that they frequently suffer.

While some of these illegal immigrants arrived from Central and South America via eastern port cities, the great majority crossed

121

the 2,000 mile border between the United States and Mexico. Some of these Mexican illegals are smuggled through checkpoints undetected, but the majority either overstay the temporary permits on which they originally legally entered the country, or simply crossed the border at some unpatrolled point. Lured by wages that are far higher than those in Mexico, they migrate to the cities where they can blend into the Chicano community and obtain employment. United States policies have alternately discouraged, encouraged, or ignored the flow of Mexican labor into the country, depending on the health of the American economy and the need for cheap agricultural labor. In recent years despite stepped up efforts to halt the flow of illegal immigrants, the numbers entering the country have apparently increased. While there are, of course, no accurate statistics, one common estimate of the number of Mexican illegals entering the country annually assumes that for every illegal apprehended and returned to Mexico by the Immigration and Naturalization Service another goes undetected. By this measure, an average of 1.4 million illegals entered the country in 1974 and 1975, double the rate of the preceeding five years. Using this assumed rate of entrants, the number of illegals residing in the country may be from 2 to 4 million.

Because most illegal aliens enter the country to obtain work, and because they are considered willing and able employees, the great majority of illegal aliens do find employment. And despite the fact that nine of ten have less than six years of schooling and speak no English, the work which they obtain is not solely menial minimum-wage jobs. Surveys of apprehended illegals have estimated the proportion employed in farm work at only about one-third, with substantial fractions finding work in manufacturing, construction, and services. This wide range of jobs means that some workers obtain relatively good wages. Although the average hourly wage reported in a 1975 survey of apprehended illegals was only $2.34, half of the illegals caught in Chicago in early 1975 reportedly earned $3.50 or more. While this average may be high, it does suggest that some illegals hold relatively good jobs.

Large numbers of illegal aliens in the labor force and the evidence that they are penetrating a broad range of industries and occupations present a policy dilemma during periods of high national unemployment. Clearly, if there are as many as 3 million illegals working in the country, many of them are holding jobs that could be otherwise filled by some of the nation's unemployed. Because illegals are often willing to work hard under adverse conditions for low wages, they tend to depress wage rates, slow improvements in working conditions, and hamper unionization efforts in agricultural and manufacturing industries, particularly in the southwestern states where they are concentrated. Moreover, while illegals themselves may have little access to unemployment insurance, welfare, or other social benefits, their impact on unemployment and wage rates doubtless forces some individuals, who would otherwise have a job to support themselves, to depend on the government for support.

Because of these adverse impacts on the welfare of the American workers there have been attempts to strengthen immigration laws. In addition to stepped up efforts by the Immigration and Naturalization Service, bills introduced in Congress have proposed that employers who hire illegals be penalized (currently there are no sanctions on hiring illegal aliens). At the same time, however, agricultural and industrial interests who claim that there is a shortage of workers willing to take low-level, low-wage jobs have advocated more lenient immigrant policies. Whatever measures are adopted, the difficulties of controlling illegal immigration will remain as long as American borders are relatively open and there are economic incentives for poor Mexicans and other nationalities to seek higher-wage U. S. jobs.

AREA DEVELOPMENT PROGRAMS

Poverty tends to become concentrated in specific geographic locations. Declining employment opportunities, high rates of out-migration, the absence of jobs for potential secondary family workers, changes in industry-mix, underdeveloped infrastructure, low educational attainment, and large proportions of farm population interact in some localities to produce so-called "depressed areas." The areas themselves vary. Poverty pockets exist in otherwise prosperous metropolitan areas, in underdeveloped rural areas, and in isolated or stagnating regions cut off from the rest of the economy. Some are as small as an inner-city neighborhood and some as expansive as Indian reservations or major sections of the Appalachian region. The problems faced by the rural and urban areas differ, but are related. The out-migration plaguing many rural areas has resulted in an influx of unskilled migrants into the cities, whose middle and upper classes in turn have fled to the suburbs. Also, depressed urban and rural areas fail to attract new economic enterprise because they frequently lack adequate public facilities. Also, the labor force tends to be deficiently educated and poorly trained.

The Public Works and Economic Development Act (EDA) of 1965, the Department of Agriculture's Rural Electrification and Telephone program, the Appalachian Regional Development Act (ARDA), and the Model Cities program authorized by the Demonstration Cities and Metropolitan Development Act of 1966, were the major federal tools for area redevelopment during the 1960s (table 9).

Table 9. Federal aid to lagging areas, 1975

Program	Outlays (millions)
Total	$2,107
Appalachian Regional Commission	311
Economic Development Administration	264
Rural Electrification Administration	496
Model Cities	345[a]
Bureau of Indian Affairs	691

Source: U.S. Office of Management and Budget

[a] Program absorbed January 1, 1975. Figure shows obligations for fiscal 1975.

The Economic Development Administration of the Department of Commerce provides labor surplus counties with grants for public works and other redevelopment projects, technical assistance and research and development grants, as well as industrial development loans and guarantees. Since the available funds are spread thinly, it is difficult to ascertain the magnitude of improvements and if they would have occurred without federal subsidy. During 1975 EDA obligated over $177 million for 285 public works grants and over $27.2 million for 31 business loans.

Since 1936, the Department of Agriculture has administered a special form of capital investment assistance to rural areas. The Rural Electrification Administration finances subsidized loans for construction and operation of generator plants, for acquisition and installation of electrical wiring and equipment by consumers, and for the improvement and expansion of the rural telephone service.

Community development aid is in the form of block grants to state and local governments for supporting initiatives aimed at stabilizing and improving housing for the poor in particular, and the community in general. The block grant approach authorized by the Housing and Community Development Act of 1974 allows state and local jurisdictions to exercise their discretion in supporting a variety of urban renewal and community improvement and development activities. After Model Cities ended in January 1975 many of the employment and training activities related to the community development were continued under the HCDA block grants, while others were carried on under the aegis of EDA in the Department of Commerce. With the growing emphasis on federal block grants and local decisionmaking, communities are expected to further integrate employment projects under the 1973 Comprehensive Employment and Training Act and community development projects under HCDA and EDA.

Continuing support for rural areas by the Department of Agriculture was authorized by the Rural Development Act of 1972. That act included budget authorizations for loans and grants for commercial and economic development and for the construction of community facilities.

The Appalachian Regional Development Act of 1965 provides a broad range of assistance programs to a 13-state area from New York to Mississippi. It is the only economic development plan to rely on a regional planning commission to channel federal funds into the area. The Public Works and Economic Development Act provided for the establishment of other regional development planning commissions, but these were never funded.

Reflecting the underlying assumption of the legislation that the economic distress of the Appalachian region is due in large part to its relative isolation (and possibly because the several states involved could initially agree on relatively few concrete projects), 59 percent of the $2.5 billion Congress appropriated for the Appalachian Regional Commission was allocated for the construction of a proposed 2,700 mile highway system and 1,500 miles of access roads. The rest of the money is used to increase the federal share in grant programs, to finance health and child-development projects, to create vocational education facilities, and to restore the land ruined by mining and for other public facilities.

Quite obviously, jobs were created by these direct expenditures; but the long-term effect of improved transportation and infrastructure in attracting industry to the region is not clear. Nor is it possible to determine whether the improvements have resulted from the healthy national economy or from the development efforts. However, the improvements in the Appalachian economy are undeniable.

Unemployment and underemployment are major contributors to poverty and deprivation in the United States. It therefore appears reasonable to consider federal measures to aid depressed areas as a part of the antipoverty effort. But a careful look at existing programs raises considerable doubt as to their effectiveness as tools in fighting poverty. This is not to say that regional and area economic rehabilitation programs are not justified on other grounds; merely that they have limited applicability in reducing poverty, at least in the short run.

The federal depressed area program essentially follows a trickle-down approach in providing incentives for businessmen to locate or to expand enterprises in depressed areas. In aiding employers and the unemployed, the program rests on the belief that federal efforts should concentrate on the business community, which, in turn, will create new jobs to help the unemployed in the future. It is a long-run strategy with little immediate antipoverty impact. Whether longer-run goals will be realized, no one can predict.

INDIAN PROGRAMS

Federal programs for American Indians are a special application of the area approach to poverty. These programs provide a wide range of goods and services as well as income and employment to Indians on reservations. This unusual concentration of federal support is a response to the serious deprivation that exists among the 543,000 Indians who live on 280 federal reservations, as well as a belated recognition of the government's culpability for the adverse conditions under which Indians live.

The highest incidence of concentrated poverty in the United States is found on Indian reservations. Comparative indicators emphasize this impoverishment. Indian families have average incomes two-fifths as large as the average American family. This lower income must be shared by families that include twice as many children under 18 as the national average. Unemployment rates on reservations are several times higher than the national average, and a majority of reservation families live in unsanitary, dilapidated housing. Moreover, the violent crime rate on reservations is nine times that for rural America; 43 percent of Indian school children, or more than double the nation's average, drop out before completing high school; and the average life span of an Indian is 6 years shorter than the national norm of 71 years. Obviously, reservation Indians desperately need a federal program that employs an area approach to their concentration of poverty.

Because of the Indians' unique historical status as wards of the state, the federal government has assumed broader responsibilities for reservation residents than for other citizens. Besides the estimated $345 million spent by various federal agencies for social welfare, and capital improvement projects on reservations, the Indian Health Service and the Bureau of Indian Affairs spent $969 million on their programs, not including funds appropriated to settle the claims of Alaskan natives or those from tribal trust funds (figure 15). This amounts to over $2,400 for each of the half million Indians residing on or near reservations. While this aid may on the surface appear to be large, it must be noted that the sources for additional funds to Indians are very limited. Lacking

127

FIGURE 15
FEDERAL ASSISTANCE TO INDIANS
1975

TOTAL - $1,314 MILLION

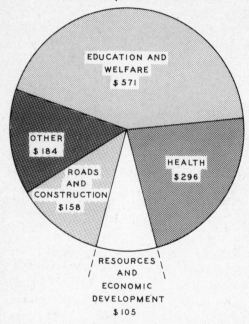

Source: U.S. Office of Management and Budget and Bureau of Indian
          Affairs

significant private resources or economic activity, Indians on reservations must depend upon federal support for essential services and goods.

Despite the relatively high per capita federal expenditures, the "big brother" approach to solving reservation problems has not worked. The reasons are complex. They include a failure to consider the Indians' cultural heritage, as well as disputes within federal agencies and among the Indians themselves regarding appropriate program goals. Paradoxically, if Indians are ever to free themselves from the federal government, even more federal aid will be necessary to develop their economic base and social institutions. Without this infrastructure, the Indian communities will be unable to contribute support to their own institutions.

ADDITIONAL READINGS

Levitan, Sar A. and Johnston, William B. *Indian Giving*. Baltimore: The Johns Hopkins University Press, 1975.

Levitan, Sar A.; Mangum, Garth L.; and Marshall, Ray. *Human Resources and Labor Markets*. New York: Harper and Row, 1976.

Levitan, Sar A. and Zickler, Joyce. *Too Little But Not Too Late: Federal Aid to Lagging Areas*. Lexington, Mass.: D. C. Heath and Lexington Books, 1976.

Levitan, Sar A.; Johnston, William B.; and Taggart, Robert. *Still A Dream*. Cambridge: Harvard University Press, 1975.

Mangum, Garth L. *Employment and Employability*. Salt Lake City, Utah: Olympus Publishing Company, 1976.

U.S. Bureau of Labor Statistics. *Youth Unemployment and Minimum Wages*. Bulletin 1657. Washington: Government Printing Office, 1970.

U.S. Department of Labor. *Employment and Training Report of the President*. Washington: Government Printing Office, current year.

6

Goals and Priorities to Combat Poverty

The needy shall not always be forgotten; the hope of the poor shall not perish for ever.

—Psalms 9:18

The Great Society's Efforts

Major strides were taken during the 1960s to combat poverty. Sustained economic growth, tight labor markets during the latter half of the decade, and the Great Society's antipoverty legislation combined to reduce poverty in the United States. These efforts, however, were not sustained. Although the Great Society's programs continued to expand and flourish during the early 1970s, national policy opted for loosening the demand for labor in order to reduce inflationary pressures.

Initiated under the Johnson administration, the rapid growth in the budget continued during the first Nixon administration. Total federal outlays more than doubled in the decade ending in 1973 and the "budget explosion" was considered to be a prime factor contributing to inflationary pressures. To reduce inflation and to cut tax burdens, the Nixon–Ford administrations focused on restraining the growth of the federal budget. Few doubted the need of constraining the expansion of federal outlays; the controversy

130

centered more on whose ox was to be gored rather than on whether any cutting was necessary.

Since programs in aid of the poor had expanded so greatly during the decade, the decision was made that much of the pruning of the budget should also be made in those programs: subsidized housing, education, manpower training programs, and related antipoverty efforts. The goal of the Great Society to eliminate poverty was abandoned as rhetoric during the second Nixon administration. Instead, the prophecy that "the poor ye shall always have with you" was readopted. Increased poverty was seen as an acceptable trade-off to check the expansion of federal budget with accompanying rising deficits and inflationary pressures.

Underlying the deemphasis of antipoverty programs was the recognition that the Great Society's hope for an easy victory over poverty remained elusive. The nation was apparently not willing to sustain the struggle against poverty as a top priority item on the American agenda. Even in this most affluent of societies the antipoverty measures must compete with other national goals. Moreover, experience from the New Deal through the 1970s made it abundantly clear that the eradication of poverty is a costly effort. National policymakers assigning a lower priority to the poor decided not to commit the resources necessary to eliminate poverty, and the administration opted instead for arresting, if not completely dismantling, the Great Society's antipoverty efforts.

The Great Society's antipoverty strategy was three-fold. First, placing emphasis upon the presumed desirability of changing the poor, the Great Society improved the provision of diverse services, focusing on educational opportunities and training. Second, the Great Society legislation aimed at changing American institutions to allow the poor a greater voice in determining their own destiny, including the planning and implementation of programs in aid of the poor. Third, the Great Society expanded direct assistance to the poor through the provision of in-kind services, including health care, shelter, and nutrition.

While diverse efforts on behalf of the poor continued to expand, the antipoverty strategy fell short of developing an orderly pro-

131

gram of providing income to the poor, although millions of poor were given additional income in a haphazard way by the expansion of public assistance, training stipends, and other measures. Congress failed to enact even the meager guaranteed income proposal of the Nixon administration.

A COMPREHENSIVE PROGRAM

A comprehensive program in aid of the poor should recognize that the poor need both income and services, not one or the other. As a reaction against the expansion of services, some antipoverty warriors have come up with a simple solution: "Give them money." While this advice will not go down in history with "Let them eat cake," it may be equally unrealistic. The provision of money alone without institutional changes and needed services will not eradicate poverty. And, given the current climate of opinion, it is not realistic to expect that society will provide enough to eliminate poverty in the foreseeable future.

A useful general rule for allocating the additional resources would be to emphasize those efforts that attack the causes of poverty rather than those which merely mitigate its symptoms. Granted that the two objectives are not easily separated, the rule suggests the need for continuing research into the factors which contribute to the persistence of poverty and a commitment to use available resources to strike at the roots of poverty.

The vast experimentation of the past dozen years suggests some courses of action for the next decade and beyond. While significant gaps remain in our understanding of the causes of poverty, we need not await returns from all the precincts to continue a vigorous campaign to reduce poverty. Lacking comprehensive knowledge, we can focus on specific measures to aid selected groups among the poor. This suggested emphasis should not necessarily supplant the generalized social goal of eliminating all poverty. A free and affluent society should aim at nothing less. We should realize that this is an ultimate goal, and one of numerous and pressing demands upon society's attentions and resources. Realistically, for the time being we must forego grand designs for the good society and concentrate on more modest and specialized strategems.

[Even assuming that consensus can be reached on the amount of additional resources to be allocated for the attack on poverty, it is not at all clear how these resources should be distributed and most effectively utilized.]What share of any additional dollars should be allocated to raising the cash income of the poor as compared with improving the quality and quantity of services that are offered to them? The poor are not a homogeneous mass. Additional income will provide for the basic needs of some; many others require services that will enable them to partake in the affluence of American society. Until these special services and income in-kind are adequate, it will be premature to hope for a guaranteed minimum income that would eliminate poverty. Indeed, in view of the multiple problems faced by the poor, it is problematic whether a reasonable cash grant can provide for their basic needs.

Guaranteed Income

Although it would be desirable to have an adequate income guarantee for all citizens in need, it is also important to note the marked improvements of our current transfer system. Even though the myriad existing programs may appear to match the confusion in the Tower of Babel, in sum they form a fairly comprehensive system. Each of the various programs has its own target group, but no longer are there major gaps in coverage.

Most recent improvements were wrought primarily by the growth of the food stamp program, by broader and longer coverage under unemployment compensation, which made significant contributions to the working poor, and by federalization of the adult public assistance categories, which improved the lot of the disabled and aged who cannot work. These substantial improvements in existing programs, however, should not be allowed to obscure the benefits of a minimal uniform national income guarantee. In keeping with the guideline that priority be given to attacking the roots of poverty, cash grants should take the form of income supplements for the working poor, work incentives for welfare recipients and other employable poor, and allowances for

133

families living in poverty. A reasonable formula would provide that the guaranteed income be, say, 70 percent of the level of income that would raise the recipient to the poverty threshold. For a family of four, in 1976 prices, this would have amounted to $3,850 per year. But a guaranteed minimum income would also require the overhauling of in-kind benefits, a difficult task at best. Moreover, in a number of states where current benefits exceed the proposed levels, equity would dictate state and local supplements above the federal contributions, further complicating the system. No one has yet designed a "neat" system to provide for the multiple needs of the poor.

Obviously, incentives would have to be provided to the poor to supplement their incomes, and to assure that the income of those who work exceeds that of the nonworking poor. This would require a graduated tax along the lines practiced by the Veterans Administration in providing pensions to indigent veterans and their dependent survivors. The exact added cost of such a plan, though difficult to estimate, would probably be less than $15 billion. This goal may be best accomplished in two or three stages, starting with an initial guaranteed income equal to 60 percent of the poverty threshold and raising the ante by 2 percent annually for five years. The slow progress in the minimum guaranteed income is necessary if society is not to neglect other commitments. Aid to the poor is only one goal of an affluent society.

Goods, Services, and Protective Legislation

While the income support program is being established and the costs are absorbed, attention should be turned to improvements in education, job training and job creation, housing, and the strengthening of protective legislation.

1. Over a century ago the people of the United States reached a consensus that free schooling should be made available to all. While publicly-supported education continually expanded, little attention was given to lowering the entry age for poor children in publicly-supported schools before the establishment of Head Start. The growing number of working women, including mothers with small children, raises the need for expanding preschool facilities on

a universal basis. Obviously it would take years and massive outlays to establish needed facilities for the more than 6 million preschool children whose mothers worked in 1975. At first, more affluent parents might be required to pay tuition to support such schools while children from poor families would be admitted free. In the field of education, then, the first priority should be given to the expansion of school facilities, starting at age four or possibly three, including the provision of day care facilities for children with working mothers.

Beyond expansion of facilities for young children, consideration must be given to improving the quality of education throughout the primary and secondary schools, particularly in poverty areas. Remedial education is extremely expensive and, to the extent that the additional investment would make the educational system more effective the first time around, it would reduce the needs for rehabilitative measures. Because a college education still remains possibly the best insurance against poverty, children from poor homes with the required intellectual capacity would benefit from special help in getting into college and obtaining financial assistance while pursuing their studies.

A college education, however, is not a feasible option for many children from poor homes who could benefit by requiring a sound basic education. A disproportionate number of poor children fail in school or are failed by the schools. No blame has to be assigned here, but it is clear that many of those who do not succeed in school on the first round will need remedial education and vocational training in order to compete effectively for gainful employment.

2. Experience has shown, however, that our economy may not generate an adequate number of jobs to gainfully employ selected sectors of the population. The poorly educated and unskilled are of particular concern to public policy, and creation of jobs for them should be second only to the establishment of adequate training facilities for those who are sufficiently motivated to acquire new skills. The continued high level of unemployment among the unskilled, particularly among blacks, indicates the need for generating government-supported employment—not make-work jobs—for

those who cannot qualify for gainful employment in private industry.

Despite the gloomy forebodings by the prophets of cybernation, much of society's needed work is not being done, and the needs are going to increase rather than disappear. Many of these jobs can be performed by relatively unskilled, unemployed workers, whether in rural areas or urban centers. Stream clearance, reforestation, and park maintenance are some of the traditional work-relief jobs. Many new jobs can be added, such as school aides, health aides, simple maintenance jobs in public buildings, and renovation of slum areas. These jobs should be in addition to countercyclical job-creation programs designed to help the victims of economic recession. Creating these jobs is costly. A program which will create 500,000 full-time jobs, not an unreasonable goal even in good times, would cost as much as $4 billion annually including outlays for materials. An even larger amount could profitably be expended to help train the unskilled and to purchase the myriad of supportive services associated with training the poor.

3. Housing for impoverished families must be given high priority because adequate low-cost shelter clearly cannot be provided by private enterprise at a profit. Housing efforts conform to Lincoln's generally accepted maxim that "the legitimate object of government is to do for the people what needs to be done, but which they cannot, by individual effort, do at all, or do so well, for themselves." Because adequate housing for the poor will remain in very short supply, priority in allocation should be given to the working poor. This judgment is not necessarily based on the assumption that the working poor are more "deserving," but flows from more pragmatic considerations. The working poor can contribute more to the cost of housing and will face less opposition from opponents of the welfare state who resist any attempt to subsidize the "indolent." The housing subsidy may also serve as an additional incentive for the poor to supplement their welfare income.

4. It would be misleading, however, to measure antipoverty efforts solely in terms of direct expenditures. The most promising way of reducing poverty is to help the poor control the size of their families. This can be achieved at negligible cost to the public.

Primary emphasis should be placed on helping the impoverished to plan parenthood and thus reduce the number of unwanted children.

Other programs that may bring the greatest returns in a concerted attack on poverty also require modest financial resources. For example, consumer education may, in the long run, help the poor more than costly food subsidies. Of greater significance would be an effective campaign to reduce—and hopefully obliterate—discrimination practiced against minorities, particularly blacks. The Civil Rights Act of 1964, the Voting Rights Act of 1965, and related executive orders, if properly enforced, could turn out to be more important tools to secure equal rights for minorities and to combat discrimination and poverty than other legislation involving huge expenditures.

Similarly, minimum wage legislation, to which no price tag can be attached, may be a more significant tool in the war on poverty than the expenditure of billions under other programs. But this must remain a limited weapon, since the boost in minimum wages also tends to reduce employment even though this negative effect cannot be measured.

A MATTER OF PRIORITIES

The foregoing list of priorities omits many needs which have persuasive claims upon available resources. In some cases, omissions are justified on practical grounds. In other cases, the choices are normative. For example, this list of priorities fails to provide additional expenditures for health care. The omission reflects the judgment that the recent rapid expansion of Medicare and Medicaid has taxed available medical facilities and services. While additional health care for poor children is sorely needed, any major attempt to further expand medical services to the poor during the next few years would probably necessitate the redistribution of existing resources. Such an effort is more likely to result in continued inflation of medical costs rather than an improvement in the quantity or quality of health services. Nor should the health needs of the nonpoor be neglected. Further major improvements of public health care, therefore, should assign first priority to the more effective delivery of health care services to the majority whose needs have not been served.

The priorities also fail to include expanded assistance for the aged, other than that required by increases in the cost of living. Hard choices must be made, and it may be anticipated that the politically potent older citizens will exercise the pressure needed to raise their social security benefits. This remains the most effective antipoverty tool in aid of aged poor.

Even in the most affluent of societies, difficult and unpleasant choices must be made among a multitude of public needs and goals. Leonard Lecht, who has carefully studied the prospects for realizing our public aspirations, concluded in his book, *The Dollar Cost of Our National Goals*, that

we could well afford the cost of any single goal at levels reflecting current aspirations, and we could probably afford the cost for any group of goals over the next decade. We could rebuild our cities, or abolish poverty, or replace all the obsolete plants and equipment in private industry, or we could begin to develop the hardware to get us to Mars and back before the year 2000. We could make some progress on all the goals, perhaps substantial progress on many, but we cannot accomplish all our aspirations at the same time.

Clearly priorities will have to be set among competing national goals. For a while during the Great Society period it appeared that the nation had made a commitment to eradicate poverty. Support for the drive was not sustained, however, and it is not likely that society will decide in the foreseeable future to commit resources adequate to eliminate poverty.

The proposed modest priorities outlined here would carry a price tag of about $25 billion, and would involve an increase of about 50 percent of all public and private outlays in aid of the poor. This increase could certainly be achieved within a decade, and perhaps in a much shorter period if society assigns a greater priority to attacking poverty than it did in the mid-1970s.

Even a sustained annual boost of $2 to $3 billion a year in antipoverty funds recognizes the fact that the reduction of poverty will remain one of several societal aspirations competing for available limited resources. It represents only a modest effort in combating poverty and would result in little, if any, redistribution of income. But who can say that our priorities will not change? Who would have predicted in the 1950s that poverty and hunger would be powerful issues in the 1960s or that a Republican president would advocate an expansion of the welfare system doubling the number of persons receiving assistance? One can always hope that society will undertake a truly effective, large-scale antipoverty effort. Such a commitment would require outlays of twice the amount indicated in the priorities outlined here. American society still has the opportunity to meet the challenge voiced by Samuel Johnson over two centuries ago: "A decent provision for the poor is the true test of civilization."

ADDITIONAL READINGS

Blechman, Barry M. et al. *Setting National Priorities: The 1976 Budget.* Washington: The Brookings Institution, 1975.

Lecht, Leonard. *Changes in National Priorities During the 1960s: Their Implications for 1980.* Washington: National Planning Association, September 1972.

Levitan, Sar A.; Johnston, William B.; and Taggart, Robert. *Minorities in the United States.* Washington: Public Affairs Press, 1975.

Rivlin, Alice. *Systematic Thinking for Social Action.* Washington: The Brookings Institution, 1971.

Index

ACTION, 81
Adult Basic Education program, 107
Advisory Committee on Intergovernmental Relations, 50
Affirmative action requirements, 115
Aged poor: needs of, 9; numbers of, 7
Agriculture, U.S. Department of: estimated cost of a minimum diet, 2; food stamp beneficiaries, 75, 76. *See also* Food stamps
Aid to Families with Dependent Children (AFDC): administration of, 27; benefit levels of, 27, 29; birth control services provided by, 90, 91; child-care programs of, 94; federal contributions to, 27; growth of, 29, 31, 32; income disregards of, 33; in-kind support offered by, 62, 69, 75, 79, 84; minimum basic needs standards for, 27, 28; Supreme Court decisions affecting, 31; work incentives under, 33, 34, 84, 114, 119
Aid to the Blind (AB). *See* Supplemental Security Income program
Aid to the Permanently and Totally Disabled (APTD). *See* Supplemental Security Income program

Appalachian Regional Commission, 126
Appalachian Regional Development Act (ARDA), 124, 125
Area development programs: antipoverty impact of, 126; approach of, 124, 125, 126; cost of, 124, 125; need for, 123, 124; urban renewal as part of, 125

Basic opportunity grants, 99, 100
Birth control: antipoverty strategy of, 15, 87, 89, 136–37; attitudes toward, 89, 90; cost of, 89, 90, 91; need for, 87, 88; programs for, 90, 91
Bureau of Indian Affairs, 127

Children in poverty: care of, 92, 93; day care for, 93, 94; deceased veterans', 41, 42; education of (*see* Education for the poor); families receiving AFDC with, 27; food for, 78; incidence of, 9; large families with, 9, 31; rate of illegitimacy among, 33; special needs of, 9, 91, 92
Civil Rights Act of 1964, 114, 137

141